Student Workbook to accompany

Aproximaciones

al estudio de la literatura hispánica

Student Workbook to accompany

Aproximaciones

al estudio de la literatura hispánica

Fourth Edition

Anita J. Vogely
Binghamton University, SUNY

Boston   Burr Ridge, IL   Dubuque, IA   Madison, WI   New York   San Francisco   St. Louis
Bangkok   Bogotá   Caracas   Kuala Lumpur   Lisbon   London   Madrid   Mexico City
Milan   Montreal   New Delhi   Santiago   Seoul   Singapore   Sydney   Taipei   Toronto

McGraw-Hill Higher Education

A Division of The **McGraw-Hill** *Companies*

This is an ⬚ book.

Student Workbook to accompany Aproximaciones al estudio de la literatura hispánica

Published by McGraw-Hill, an imprint of The McGraw-Hill Companies, Inc., 1221 Avenue of the Americas, New York, NY 10020. Copyright © 2001 The McGraw-Hill Companies, Inc. All rights reserved. No part of this publication may be reproduced or distributed in any form or by any means, or stored in a data base or retrieval system, without the prior written permission of The McGraw-Hill Companies, Inc., including, but not limited to, in any network or other electronic storage or transmission, or broadcast for distance learning.

1 2 3 4 5 6 7 8 9 0 QPD QPD 0 9 8 7 6 5 4 3 2 1 0

ISBN 0-07-228477-3

Vice president/Editor-in-chief: *Thalia Dorwick*
Executive editor: *William R. Glass*
Development editor: *Becka McGuire*
Marketing manager: *Nick Agnew*
Associate project manager: *David Sutton*
Senior production supervisor: *Richard DeVitto*
Compositor: *Shepherd, Inc.*
Typeface: *Palatino*
Printer: *Quebecor Printing Dubuque, Inc.*

http:/www.mhhe.com

Contents

Preface

This new Workbook to accompany *Aproximaciones al estudio de la literatura hispánica*, Fourth Edition, has been designed to guide students in developing effective reading strategies for Hispanic literature, including narrative, poetry, drama, and essay. Introductory literature courses are typically offered after two to six semesters of language study, when many non-native Spanish-speaking students may still be grappling with the more complex linguistic structures and interpretive uses of the language. The literature course at this level is thus most effective when viewed as a transitional course in which emphasis is given to both the language and the literature. The instructor can help students make connections between the syntax, semantics, and sociolinguistic aspects of the Spanish language and the language of Spanish literature. A transitional course also allows students to create the strong cultural, linguistic, and semantic knowledge base they will need in order to move from "learning to read" to "reading to learn" (Schulz, 1981, 43).

This Workbook will help both students and instructors make that transition by providing three important elements necessary for effective learning: (1) a focus on both skill and content, (2) a structured teaching of reading comprehension strategies, and (3) sequenced tasks that guide and increase students' intellectual risk. The structured instruction of reading strategies and reflective questioning techniques guides students through the main text and helps them develop the skills that are necessary in order to "manage the richness of words which gives significance to literary works" (Yanes, 1992, 1349)—that is, the skills that will help them learn to *interpret* literature, not just read it. Sequenced strategies and tasks that guide and increase students' intellectual risk help them negotiate the information and literary selections presented in the main text in a way that reinforces their knowledge each step of the way. Hopefully, the reading and interpretation of Spanish literature becomes a pleasurable undertaking and an exciting challenge, rather than a tedious and overwhelming task.

HOW TO USE THIS WORKBOOK

You will notice right away that the Workbook is written in English. Its purpose is not to teach the Spanish language but to provide students with concrete skills for reading literary texts. However, any of the students' work can be done in Spanish. Furthermore, instructors can translate tasks and exercises into Spanish to use in the classroom, should they desire.

The chapters in the Workbook correspond directly with those in the main text. The introduction to each genre is broken into manageable sections, providing tasks designed to help students extract pertinent information and document that information with the help of graphic organizers. (Samples of the graphic organizers are provided in the Appendix so that students can make copies as necessary and use them throughout their study of literature.) Once students have completed the introduction to a genre, the Workbook guides students through a sequence of reading stages and strategies by applying them to an example literary selection from the relevant chapter in the main text. These stages and strategies—which form the heart of this approach—are designed to help students develop effective reading comprehension techniques. Both native and non-native Spanish speakers will benefit from this approach.

As readers, students must participate actively in the reading process. At some point, they might feel overwhelmed by the density of the language in the text and the number of tasks, stages, and strategies presented in the Workbook. This is natural. For non-native speakers it can be frustrating not to be able to read Spanish with the same ease with which they read their native language. This Workbook will provide students with the appropriate tools to negotiate and regulate their self-learning in order to develop the skills necessary to interpret and appreciate Spanish literature.

SPECIAL FEATURES OF THE WORKBOOK

 This icon indicates that the task or activity refers directly to a section in the main text. Students are expected to go to the main text and complete the task or activity based on the indicated section.

When this icon appears, the task or activity is to be completed in study groups, although certain ones could also be used effectively during class. Students are encouraged to form study groups outside of class.

Test Yourself: This recurring task gives students the opportunity to self-test the information and skills they have acquired after completing a set of tasks.

Study Hint: Each chapter contains at least one Study Hint, activities that help students master particularly useful, or complicated, reading strategies. They are designed to expand students' interaction with the genre under study.

ACKNOWLEDGMENTS

Although the name of only one author appears on the cover of a book, it actually takes a legion of people to make it happen. Because of limited space, I can mention only a few of the people without whose support and assistance I could not have accomplished this feat. The first acknowledgment in anything I do goes to my parents and their unfailing belief in me as a person. I thank my husband, Dana, for bringing me coffee in bed at 5:30 every morning; my mentor, E. George Erdman, Jr., who supported me from start to finish; and my friend and colleague Kathy Martinez, who read and reread, commented, and encouraged throughout the process. Most of all, I thank my daughter Leah, who is the light of my life.

It almost goes without saying that I also thank the coauthors of *Aproximaciones al estudio de la literatura hispánica*—Carmelo Virgillo, Teresa Valdivieso, and Edward Friedman—without whom none of this ever could have happened. And, finally, thanks go to the staff at McGraw-Hill—Thalia Dorwick, William R. Glass, David Sutton, and Becka McGuire—who helped my idea become a reality.

REVIEWERS

Sol Miguel-Prendes, Wake Forest University
América Martínez-Lewis, University of Delaware

References and Select Bibliography

Armstrong, Thomas. 1994. *Multiple Intelligences in the Classroom.* Alexandria, VA: Association for Supervision and Curriculum Development.

Bacon, Wallace and Robert S. Breene. 1961. *Literature for Interpretation.* New York: Holt, Rinehart, and Winston.

Costa, Arthur. 1988. Personal communication with Jane M. Healy in *Endangered Minds* (1990). New York: Simon & Schuster.

Gardner, Howard. 1983. *Frames of Mind: The Theory of Multiple Intelligences.* New York: Basic Books.

Goldman, Daniel. 1995. *Emotional Intelligence.* New York: Bantam Books.

Harper, Sandra. 1988. "Strategies for Teaching Literature at the Undergraduate Level." *The Modern Language Journal 72:* 402–8.

Kramsch, Claire. 1985. "Literary Texts in the Classroom: A Discourse Model." *The Modern Language Journal 65:* 43–53.

Mamchur, Carolyn. 1996. *A Teacher's Guide to Cognitive Type Theory & Learning Style.* Alexandria, VA: Association for Supervision and Curriculum Development.

Nance, Kimberly A. 1994. "Developing Student's Sense of Literature in the Introductory Foreign Language Literature Course." *Association of Departments of Foreign Languages Bulletin 25:* 23–29.

Oxford, Rebecca. 1990. *Language Learning Strategies: What Every Teacher Should Know.* Boston: Heinle & Heinle Publishers.

——— and Roberta Lavine. 1992. "Teacher-student Style Wars in the Language Classroom: Research Insights and Suggestions." *Association of Departments of Foreign Languages Bulletin 23.2:* 38–45.

Schank, Roger C. and Robert P. Abelson. 1997. *Scripts, Plans, Goals, and Understandings.* Hillsdale, NJ: Erlbaum.

Schulz, Renate A. 1981. "Literature and Readability: Bridging the Gap in Foreign Language Reading." *The Modern Language Journal 65:* 43–53.

Yanes, Jeanne M. 1992. "Comprehensible Input via Culture-Schema: Preparation and Inspiration for Literary Study." *Hispania 75:* 1348–54.

Young, Dolly J. and Darlene Wolf. 1994. *Esquemas,* 2d Ed. Ft. Worth, TX: Rinehart and Winston.

DEDICATION

This book is dedicated to the memory of three incredible women:
Sharon Hamilton Ennis
Constance Coiner
Darlene Wolf

INTRODUCCIÓN: GETTING STARTED

In the introduction to *Aproximaciones al estudio de la literatura hispánica*, Fourth Edition, the authors state that literature, as an artistic creation, **"lleva consigno una nueva visión de la vida y del mundo que nos rodea."** The purpose of this Workbook is to guide you in your exploration of the literary selections in the main text, through which you will seek this "new vision of life and the world that surrounds us." The Workbook does this by providing structured tasks designed to help you develop effective reading comprehension strategies. The structured approach is presented through a series of stages and strategies in which you first build the background knowledge necessary to read and interpret narratives, poetry, drama, and essays, and then apply this knowledge to a sample selection in each genre. By developing effective reading skills in a structured fashion, eventually you will become a self-sufficient reader. The Workbook is designed so that you can use it outside of class—either alone or in groups—or as part of the classroom experience. It provides self-tests, study hints, and ideas for organizing information that correspond directly to the information presented in the main text.

The stages and strategies in this Workbook reflect a process of exploration that builds on itself. To avoid being overwhelmed by the amount of information presented, you will learn to break it down into manageable sections that relate to the genres, writers, strategies, and tasks you are studying, then to put it all back together into a cohesive whole. Think of it as though you were assembling a complex jigsaw puzzle.

Before you embark on this literary adventure in Spanish, take some time to think about and jot down some thoughts about the following questions and statements. This will prepare you for the challenges that may lie ahead and cue you to effective ways to meet those challenges.

1. *What is your experience with and attitude toward learning in general?* Has learning been easy or difficult for you? Do you believe that learning should "happen" without focused, sustained effort? Are you concerned that you will not be able to do the level of work required? If you do not understand something the first time, do you work with it until you figure it out or do you accept not knowing and go on?

    _____

    _____

    _____

    _____

    _____

2. *What kind of background do you have in reading Spanish, or English, literature and literary criticism?* Have you taken any literary criticism courses? Do you believe that you are fluent enough to be able to comprehend the Spanish texts when you read them? Do you feel prepared to tackle the language and vocabulary characteristic of literature? Does the thought of reading poetry in Spanish leave you feeling overwhelmed?

    _____

    _____

    _____

    _____

    _____

3. ***Are you familiar with your own style of learning?*** Do you prefer to think out loud, or to yourself? Do you work better in a group or alone? Do you retain information longer if you read it or if you hear it? Are you better with broad abstract concepts, or with specific details and sequences of events?

_____

_____

_____

_____

_____

_____

Why are these questions important? Consider the following statements.

1. ***What is your experience with and attitude toward learning in general?*** Your attitude will set the stage for success. Students with a positive attitude toward and experience with learning tend to think episodically, actively drawing on and applying past experiences to the issue at hand; they persevere in the face of challenges; they avoid responding impulsively and carefully consider all possible answers; they formulate ideas and support those ideas with knowledge; they are open to the ideas of others and can engage in honest discussion. Do you share these experiences and attitudes? According to Daniel Goldman (1995), hope, optimism, and positive thinking are the greatest predictors of academic success. By adopting this attitude, the literary studies you are about to pursue will become an exciting adventure.

2. ***What kind of background do you have in reading Spanish, or English, literature and literary criticism?*** Remember to relate the concepts you have learned through other courses or studies to what you are learning in this one. If you enter the introductory course feeling that you do not really know how to read literature as an art form, you may be uncomfortable tackling the technical vocabulary, strategies, and critical concepts involved in reading lengthy literary texts that frequently contain abstract and intimidating vocabulary and linguistic structures. Are you intimidated by Spanish literature? If so, re-read the answer to the first question—attitude is everything!

3. ***Are you familiar with your own style of learning?*** *How* people learn is just as important as *what* they learn. Knowing what your personal learning preferences are will help you determine the strategies that will be most helpful to you in the learning process. Experimentation is the one way to uncover those preferences. Another way is to explore the research on learning styles and strategies yourself or find someone who can introduce you to them. You are ultimately responsible for your own learning. Take charge of it and learn to recognize how you learn best. Focus on what you do know and can do, rather than on what you do not know or cannot do. Always remember, your most powerful learning tool has little to do with how smart you are, and everything to do with *how* you are smart (Gardner, 1983).

General Tips and Strategies for Students in an Introductory Spanish Literature Course

- Designate a binder or folder, with pockets, for each genre you study (narrative, poetry, and so forth). Keep all your work on the genre in this folder.
- Make multiple copies of any graphic organizer that works for you. A graphic organizer is a structure designed to help you organize information in a nonlinear way. Examples of graphic

organizers are word wheels, venn diagrams, and star diagrams. A sample of each graphic organizer presented in the Workbook is provided in the Appendix for you to copy and use as necessary.

- Always make a copy of the literary text you are studying to use as your "working copy," and include it in your binder or folder for the genre. Use it to make notes to yourself, circle, highlight, and so on. That way you always have a clean copy of the text to refer to. In this Workbook, you will be instructed to do all of your work on a working copy of the text you are studying.

- Maintain an ongoing vocabulary list for useful transition words, literary terminology, adjectives, time phrases, and other words and expressions that help you understand what you are reading.

- A good first step when approaching a new selection is to *skim* the text for the main idea. Look it over quickly to get a general idea of what it is about in order to predict what it will contain before you read it more closely. When you skim, you do not read word for word; rather, you look at the title, subtitles, key words, cognates, grammatical elements, and other information that will enable you to extract the gist and anticipate the main ideas and themes.

- Next, *scan* the text for specific information that will explain, expand, elaborate on, or add to your general understanding of the main idea. The information you are seeking will be determined by the purpose of the task.

- While skimming and/or scanning a text, write down any and all of your thoughts and ideas. Do not reject any ideas at this point. You can cull them later, if necessary; sometimes the ideas you think are weakest end up being the most insightful.

- Practice paraphrasing the information you gathered through skimming and scanning. This will help you express the information in your own words.

- Even if you prefer to work alone, establish a study group in the first week of classes and meet regularly throughout the semester. Sharing ideas with other students helps you expand your own understanding.

- Try to speak only Spanish during your study group—this will be challenging at first, but will pay off in the long run. Ultimately you will need to speak and write about Spanish literature in Spanish. Actively using Spanish in your study group will strengthen and expand your vocabulary and your ability to express your ideas in Spanish. It is also an opportunity to take safe risks.

- Discuss *how* you got an answer, not just the answer you got. When you understand how you arrived at an answer, you can change the thinking process that you used to come up with that answer. For instance, errors sometimes stem from a misinterpretation of a word or a phrase; being able to pinpoint the source of an error helps you build your skills as a learner and problem solver.

- Save all of your work so that you can refer to it during group or class discussions.

- Keep in mind that reading in a foreign language is not a linear process: you cannot simply read the text once through and expect to comprehend it fully. People do read linearly in their native language, because their comprehension of the language is so much more extensive. In a foreign language, however, you must read and re-read the text to build a knowledge structure and to confirm comprehension. The more often you work with the text, the greater your understanding of it will be.

Stages and Strategies for Reading Spanish Literature: An Overview

Objective:

- To gain an overview of the four stages of reading and the related strategies that will be developed in this Workbook

In this text you will study four literary genres: narrative, poetry, drama, and essay. The strategies in reading Stages I and II presented in this Workbook are the same for all four genres. However, due to the physical structure of poetry and the textual analysis skills required to read it with comprehension, the strategies in Stages III and IV differ for poetry.

With every genre, the first stages and strategies are just as important as the last. They are designed as a sequence, to be done in order from first to last with each text that you read. Take care not to skip or rush through the earlier ones because you consider them unnecessary. Think of it as an investment: As your reading skills become more proficient, you will be able to condense several strategies and you will read more quickly and with greater comprehension.

STAGE I. DEVELOP CULTURAL/HISTORICAL FRAMEWORK

Objectives:

- To increase background knowledge of the time and place in which an author wrote
- To uncover information about the writer, poet, dramatist, or essayist that offers clues as to the significance of the selection(s) under study

Your study of literature in any genre should begin by developing what is called a "cultural schema." This is a knowledge structure or stereotyped sequence of actions that offers a cultural, and often historical, context to a specific epoch, and provides intertextual elements to the literary works of that time (Schank & Abelson 1997; Yanes 1992; Nance 1994). With a cultural/historical framework, you, the reader, can relate to and understand more easily the thoughts, circumstances, concepts, attitudes, and attributes presented in the text you are about to study. Sources for cultural/historical knowledge can include children's literature, folklore, songs, historical or dramatic references, movies, slides, videos, magazines, newspapers, the World Wide Web, the MLA Bibliography, and various CD-ROMs, among others. The more input you gather, the stronger your cultural/historical knowledge base will be.

The strategies in Stage I help you explore, discover, and document the information you gather on the culture and history of each text and writer. As you add new genres and writers to the framework, you can begin to establish relationships between and among the writers you study, which will provide you with a global perspective of Spanish literature and its place in the "new vision of life and the world that surrounds us."

Strategy 1. Create Graphic Organizer
Strategy 2. Expand Background Knowledge
Strategy 3. Use Textbook as Resource

STAGE II. PRE-READING OBSERVATIONS

Objective:

- To make observations and predictions about the text using words and phrases as clues to meaning

Your goal in Stage II is to actively engage your mind with the literary text, by skimming and scanning for clues that will establish its purpose and help you predict its meaning. Using these clues and your cultural/historical framework from Stage I, you will explore the text and speculate on what you might learn from it. Certain words and phrases will suggest a context, which may or may not be correct, and the context in turn will trigger information about similar situations you may have experienced, read about, or heard about. The results of your pre-reading observations will provide the basis for free association exercises. Stay open-minded and generate as many ideas as possible. The ideas that are relevant can be determined later; here quantity, rather than quality, is the focus.

Strategy 1. Make Working Copy of Text
Strategy 2. Brainstorm About Title
Strategy 3. Skim Text for Main Idea
Strategy 4. Brainstorm and Speculate

STAGE III. FIRST READING FOR NARRATIVE, DRAMA, AND ESSAY

Objective:

- To scan for specific grammatical and textual elements that provide basic information about the text

The information you gather in this stage builds on the information from Stages I and II. Keeping in mind the cultural/historical flavor of the text and the main idea, in this stage you will scan the text for information about specific questions. The text is broken into segments so that you can explore and document the different elements of which each genre is composed. The strategies in Stage III will help you develop your fact-finding skills.

> **Strategy 1. Analyze First and Final Segments**
> **Strategy 2. Scan Each Segment for Information**
> **Strategy 3. Create Word Wheel for Each Character**
> **Strategy 4. Complete Star Diagram with Answers to the "Five W's"**
> **Strategy 5. Identify Information Gaps**

STAGE III. FIRST READING FOR POETRY

Objective:

- To analyze the versification (**la versificación**) of a poem based on its physical structure

This stage targets the specific textual-analysis skills required to read poetry. The strategies focus first on identifying the poem based on its smallest denominator, the syllable, and then work through the verses and stanzas until the focus is the poem itself. Once you have identified the poetic elements and classified the poem, you will then search the poem for answers to specific questions.

> **Strategy 1. Classify Verses**
> **Strategy 2. Determine Type and Pattern of Rhyme**
> **Strategy 3. Identify Type of Poem**
> **Strategy 4. Scan Each Segment for Information**
> **Strategy 5. Identify Information Gaps**

STAGE IV. SECOND READING FOR NARRATIVE, DRAMA, AND ESSAY

Objective:

- To create a thematic structure based on the text in order to determine what happens to whom

The goal of this stage is to create a thematic structure based on the literary devices pertinent to the selection, for example, **la historia, el discurso,** and **el tema.** The thematic structure traces the development of **la historia** by documenting **el desarrollo, el punto decisivo,** and **el desenlace** of the text. With your pre-reading observations and the facts you found in the first reading, you will discover "who does what to whom" and explore the surface meaning of the text by breaking it down into its component parts and reconstructing it within a thematic structure.

> **Strategy 1. Review Relevant Syntax**
> **Strategy 2. Relate Actions to Characters**
> **Strategy 3. Summarize Each Segment**
> **Strategy 4. Create Thematic Structure**

STAGE IV. SECOND READING FOR POETRY

Objective:

- To create a thematic structure of the poem by identifying the types of literary language and syntax it uses

Your goal here is to focus specifically on the language and syntax of the poem in order to determine the poem's purpose and meaning. These strategies are designed to prepare you to interpret the poetic images and literary language of the poem.

> **Strategy 1. Identify Literary Language**
> **Strategy 2. Analyze Syntax**
> **Strategy 3. Summarize Each Segment**
> **Strategy 4. Create Thematic Structure**

NOTE: At this point you may be feeling overwhelmed by the stages and strategies just presented. That is natural. It can be frustrating not to be able to read in a foreign language with the same ease as in one's native language. This Workbook will help you develop and practice effective reading strategies so that you can strengthen your ability to read and comprehend Spanish literature. Your goal is to apply and practice these strategies so that you go to your Spanish literature course an informed reader, ready and able to make valuable contributions to the class discussions. Know that you can read to learn, just as you learned to read. Keep in mind the following Study Hint as you work through the stages and strategies presented in this Workbook.

Study Hint: Reading to Learn

1. Always read with an objective or a purpose, that is, in search of some kind of information or clue to the meaning of the text.
2. True comprehension takes time and energy. Remember that reading for comprehension is a recursive process and must be approached strategically. You must put time and energy into developing your reading skills.
3. No text exists in a vacuum. There is always a greater cultural/historical context that impacts the meaning of the text. Always read a text through a global lens.
4. As the reader, you must participate actively in the reading process. The stages and strategies in this Workbook are designed to maximize your participation and interaction with the text. Make connections, speculate, elaborate, and question. Take advantage of the learning opportunity.

¡Buena suerte!

Task 3. Practice. With your study group, do the **Práctica** section on pages 19–24 of the text. Remember to discuss *how* you arrive at your answers, and not just the answers themselves.

B. PANORAMA HISTÓRICO

Objectives:

- To extract pertinent information about the specific writers you will study in this course
- To place the specific selections of the anthology within the overall context of Hispanic literature

The tasks in this section will help you extract pertinent information about the specific writers you will be studying. This is going to be a large amount of information. Do not try to digest it all at the beginning of the course or you will be overwhelmed. Be patient, process it one piece at a time, within the framework of your syllabus, and eventually you will be able to put the whole puzzle together in a meaningful way.

EL GÉNERO NARRATIVO: DEFINICIÓN Y ORÍGENES

Task 1. Skim and Scan. Skim the overview of the narrative on pages 24–25 of the text to get the gist of the information it provides. Then scan for answers to the following questions, making note of the paragraph(s) and sentence(s) in which the information appears.

1. What kind of information does this section provide? _____

_____

_____

2. What is the origin of the word *narrative*? _____

_____

_____

3. What is the definition of the narrative? _____

_____

_____

4. How does a writer use the narrative as a tool of expression? _____

_____

_____

Task 2. Identify Key Words. If you were to pursue further research on the narrative genre, what are some key words from the paragraph in Task 1 that might assist in a computer or library search? Jot them down here.

_____   _____

_____   _____

_____   _____

NOTE: Since *La camisa de Margarita* is the sample narrative used in the Stages and Strategies for Reading Narratives, the next step is to read about the specific time in which Ricardo Palma lived and wrote. According to the introduction to the story (pp. 42–43), Palma was born in Lima, Peru, and lived from 1833 to 1919.

Task 3. Scan for Information. Scan the section entitled **El romanticismo en la narrativa hispanoamericana** on page 30 for answers to the following questions.

1. With which politically driven developments did the emergence of **el romanticismo hispanoamericano** coincide?

_____

_____

2. What literary genre dominated this period? According to the authors, why was this genre so popular?

_____

_____

3. What are the five categories of the genre mentioned in this section, the principal writers in each, and an example text?

Category	Principal Writers	Example Text

Task 4. Summarize. The section entitled **Dos géneros americanos: lo «gauchesco» y la «tradición»** (pp. 30–31) specifically addresses the role that Ricardo Palma played in the emergence of a strictly Latin American novel. Summarize his contribution to this literary movement.

_____

_____

_____

Task 5. Test Yourself. Before you continue, make sure that you can answer the following questions without referring to your notes.

1. What kind of information does a historical panorama provide to the reader of literature? What kinds of insights into a literary movement does this type of perspective provide?

2. What are the connections between literature and history?

3. Can you place the writer you are studying into the literary movement(s) of his/her time? What did that writer contribute to the literary movement(s)?

4. How does the writer's contribution relate to what came before and what followed?

5. If you were to do further research on the writer being studied, what key words might you use to find information?

C. STAGES AND STRATEGIES FOR READING NARRATIVES

Objectives:

- To use the Stage I strategies to build a cultural/historical framework for the narratives to be read, in particular *La camisa de Margarita* by Ricardo Palma
- To apply the reading comprehension strategies in Stages II, III, and IV to Palma's story

Remember that the purpose of this section is to develop stages and strategies for reading narratives for comprehension. This is a process that builds on itself. It is therefore important that you spend the necessary time on each stage; with practice you will be able to combine stages and strategies to maximize your comprehension of the text you are reading.

Stage I. Develop Cultural/Historical Framework

As you learned in the **Introducción:** Getting Started, the first step is to construct a cultural/historical framework, beginning here with the narratives you will read in this course. Building this structure for the first time will require intensive thought, planning, and work. As you continue your study of literature, however, you will update and expand, not re-create, the cultural/historical framework. For this reason, it is critical that the structure you create be flexible enough to accommodate new information. The more time you spend on this phase the first time, the less you will spend later.

STRATEGY 1. CREATE GRAPHIC ORGANIZER

A graphic organizer is any visual aid, such as the venn diagrams and charts you created earlier in this chapter, that helps you organize and document ideas and information so that you can make intelligent guesses and/or predictions about a text. It can take many forms, but above all it must be meaningful to you, and it must be open and flexible enough that you can add new information as you discover it.

The content of the graphic organizer will depend on what you are studying. In this case, you need a way to organize the cultural and historical information that is most relevant to the writers you will study in this course. For example, following page 398 of the main text, the authors have included a chronological index of historical events and the specific texts written in each genre around the time of those events. This graphic organizer provides an excellent model to follow (see Appendix for a blank chart), or you can create a different type. The structure can change and evolve as the course progresses and as you begin to study other genres.

Task 1. Create Graphic Organizer. Decide what kind of graphic organizer you are going to use—a chart, a time line, a chronological index—and create a broad, comprehensive overview of the centuries and genres of the selections you will be reading. Make sure to build your chart *based on the selections that your instructor has selected for study in this course.*

 Task 2. Collaborate. Share your graphic organizer with your study group and provide each other with constructive feedback.

STRATEGY 2. EXPAND BACKGROUND KNOWLEDGE

Think back on other classes you have taken that provided a historical or cultural perspective of Spain, Europe, or Latin America. You can expand your background knowledge by researching the music and art, or any other area of interest, of the epochs of the texts you are studying.

Task 1. Key Word Search. Look at the key words you listed in Task 2 of **Panorama histórico** (p. 11). Use at least three of them within a broader category—for example, art and architecture—to do a computer and/or library search. Relate the words to the relevant writers and literature. Document the key words you use, the category you research, and a brief summary of the information you find.

Key Word			
Category			
Summary			

Task 2. Personal Research. Find a personal source of information (a professor, instructor, local teacher, friend, graduate student, librarian) who is interested in Hispanic history and culture, the narrative genre, the writer you are studying, or a related topic. Try to expand your knowledge base by talking to that person about the topic(s) of your research. Document your discoveries here.

1. With whom did you talk? _____

2. What did you learn? _____

_____

_____

_____

_____

_____

3. What could you do to find out more about the topic? _____

_____

_____

_____

STRATEGY 3. USE TEXTBOOK AS RESOURCE

Task 1. Transfer Information. Look at the information you documented from the **Panorama histórico** section. What pertinent information could you extract and transfer to the cultural/historical framework you created in Strategy 1?

Task 2. Scan for Key Words. Scan **Vida y obra** from the introduction to *La camisa de Margarita* on page 42 of the text, using the reading strategies you have been practicing. Note the key words and phrases. What additional information about Palma's life can you add to your cultural/ historical framework that could explain why he writes what he writes and the way he writes it?

Key words:

_____   _____

_____   _____

_____   _____

Additional information about Palma's life: _____

_____

Task 3. Scan for Key Words. Scan **El autor y su contexto** on page 43 of the text. What was life like in Peru during Palma's life? How did it influence his writing? What did Palma contribute to the literary trends of his time?

_____

_____

_____

Stage II. Pre-Reading Observations

Objective:

- To make observations and predictions about the text using words and phrases as clues to meaning

Your goal in Stage II is to engage your mind actively by searching the literary text for physical and visual clues that will establish the purpose for reading it and will help you predict its meaning. Using these clues and your own background knowledge, you will explore the text and speculate on what you might learn from it. Certain words and phrases will suggest a context, which may or may not be correct, and the context in turn will trigger information about similar situations you may have experienced, read about, or heard about. The results of your pre-reading observations will then provide the basis for free association exercises. Stay open to all possibilities. Here quantity of thought is the goal; correctness of thought can be determined later.

NOTE: Always keep your cultural/historical framework at hand. Remember that the authors of *Aproximaciones* selected every text for a reason, and part of your job is to determine that reason. Who is the writer of the selection and where does he/she fit into the cultural/historical framework? Where does his/her writing style fit into the literary trends of the age? What did he/she contribute?

STRATEGY 1. MAKE WORKING COPY OF TEXT

Task 1. Create Working Copy. Photocopy the selection you are reading (in this case, *La camisa de Margarita* on pp. 43–45 of the text). Do all of your work on the photocopy so that you always have a clean copy of the selection to read in the textbook.

Task 2. Segment Text. Divide the text into segments of about 20 lines, or where it seems natural, and number each segment. (Generally, between 12 to 15 segments is the most effective number.) Then, on another piece of paper, write the corresponding segment numbers. Be sure to allow plenty of space to write about each segment; if possible, have no more than two segments per page. You will use this numbered paper to document observations and information about the corresponding segments.

STRATEGY 2. BRAINSTORM ABOUT TITLE

Task 1. Brainstorm. Is there an obvious word in the title that places you in a moment in time? Do the words engender certain images? Are there terms that evoke a cultural, historical, religious, or mythological reference? Does the title create a feeling or other response? Document all of your ideas on a word wheel such as the one on the next page (see Appendix for a blank one).

NOTE: The word wheel is another graphic organizer that can be used to visually represent the information generated by brainstorming. Free association activities are meant to document as many ideas as possible in one place so that you can revisit them at a later time and cull them for pertinent information.

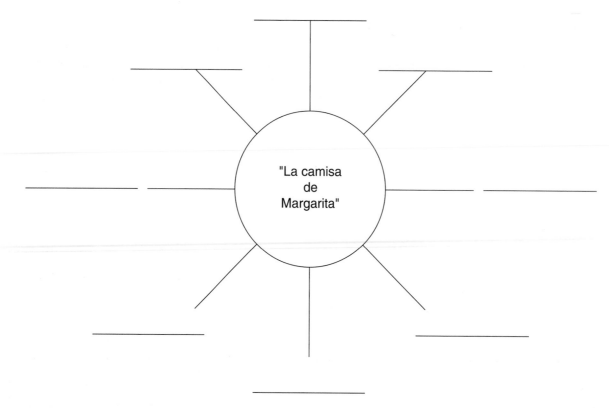

STRATEGY 3. SKIM TEXT FOR MAIN IDEA

Task 1. Skim and Document. Using your segmented working copy of the text, move from segment to segment and skim for information that might help you determine the main idea of the story. Note the names of any characters. Document all of your observations on the numbered paper you created in Strategy 1, Task 2. Pay particular attention to the glossed vocabulary words and their relevance to your comprehension of the text.

STRATEGY 4. BRAINSTORM AND SPECULATE

Task 1. Synthesize. Examine, then synthesize the information you gathered in Strategies 2 and 3. Do you notice a pattern or theme in the topic or syntax (grammar)? Based on this synthesis, brainstorm all of the possible themes that might develop in the text. Use a new word wheel to document your ideas. Write down, in English or in Spanish, the ideas as they come into your head. Do not edit or reject any idea during this activity. When you finish brainstorming, you can transpose any English you used into Spanish.

 Share the results of your brainstorm with your study group. Be sure to discuss not only what you wrote down but also the source of inspiration for your ideas. Narrow down the possibilities with the information you have gathered.

Stage III. First Reading

Objective:

- To scan for specific grammatical and textual elements that provide basic information about the narrative

This is the fact-finding stage. The primary emphasis here is on recognition of textual elements rather than strictly text comprehension. Keeping your information organized will be important.

STRATEGY 1. ANALYZE FIRST AND FINAL SEGMENTS

Task 1. Complete Fact Sheet for First Segment. Again using your segmented working copy of the text, examine the first segment. Does it relate to the title? How? What kind of tone does it set? What kind of information does it offer? What information does it *not* offer? Complete the following fact sheet with the verb tenses, the type of vocabulary, and other general information.

FACT SHEET

Title: _____

Segment # _____

Verb Tenses	Vocabulary	General Information

Additional information or observations: _____

Task 2. Complete Fact Sheet for Final Segment. Using your working copy of the text and a new fact sheet (see Appendix for a blank copy that you can reproduce), analyze the final segment. How does it relate or not relate to the first segment? What kind of closure does it offer or not offer? Note any changes of observations, whether in terms of the lexicon (vocabulary), syntax (grammar), or semantics (meaning), no matter how unimportant they may seem at this point.

STRATEGY 2. SCAN EACH SEGMENT FOR INFORMATION

Task 1. Scan for Information. Using your segmented working copy of the text and additional fact sheets, work through the remaining segments. Scan each one for vocabulary and verbs that contribute to the main idea of the text. Determine which verbs represent the main action and which verbs provide important state-of-being information. Document this information on the fact sheet. What observations can you make about the verbs? Do you see any patterns (for example, changes in the tense and/or mood of the verb)?

STRATEGY 3. CREATE WORD WHEEL FOR EACH CHARACTER

Task 1. Create Word Wheels. Based on the work you have done so far, you should have already extracted the names of any characters in the selection. Create a word wheel for each character that describes what the character is like. Be sure to include textual references and page numbers.

STRATEGY 4. COMPLETE STAR DIAGRAM WITH ANSWERS TO THE "FIVE W'S"

Task 1. Scan for Information. Scan the text and mark the words or phrases that answer the following questions.

> **Who?** The teller of the story (**el emisor / el autor / el narrador**), and the hearer of the story (**el receptor / el lector**)

> **What?** The topic or message of the text (**el mensaje / el texto / la historia**)

> **Where?** The historical and/or geographical context, or space, of the text (or the absence thereof)

> **When?** The time frame of the text

> **Why?** The purpose or meaning of the text (**el tema**)

Task 2. Complete Star Diagram. Organize the answers to the above questions on a star diagram such as the following (there is also a blank copy in the Appendix). Each "point" of the star corresponds to one of the five W's. For each point, cite the words or phrases from the text that substantiate your answer. Document all of your observations. Remember that the more observations you make of the specific elements of the text, the more likely you will be to perceive patterns, redundancies, and dominant images.

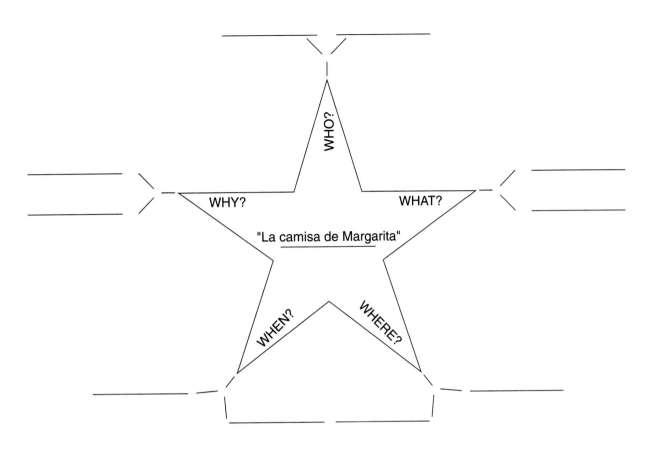

 Share your star diagram with your study group.

STRATEGY 5. IDENTIFY INFORMATION GAPS

Task 1. Review. Review what you learned about the narrative in the first part of this chapter so that you know what it is you need to know in order to understand and discuss this particular literary form.

Task 2. Identify Information Gaps. Make note of the information that you did *not* uncover during Stages II and III. The information that you do not have is just as important as the information that you do. It is fine to not know something at this point, as long as you are aware of what you do know and what you still need to know.

I know: _____

_____

_____

I need to know: _____

_____

_____

Task 3. Identify Vocabulary Gaps. List any vocabulary or concept that you do not understand. It is important to begin by trying to clarify confusion on your own. Try to guess at meaning based on root words, context, and prior knowledge about story formats and similar situations. Then consult the textbook, a dictionary, and/or another classmate. Finally, ask your instructor. Write down what you learn about each vocabulary item or concept.

_____

_____

_____

_____

Stage IV. Second Reading

Objective:

- To create a thematic structure of the text

The goal of this final stage of reading is to determine _who does what to whom or what,_ by first breaking the text down into its component parts and then putting it back together in a way that makes sense to you, the reader. When you are done you have what is known as a thematic structure, which is developed through a more extensive exploration of the surface structure, or syntax, of the text. The purpose is not to focus strictly on the grammar of the text, but to access the linguistic tools you will need to facilitate comprehension and textual interpretation.

STRATEGY 1. REVIEW RELEVANT SYNTAX

Noam Chomsky, a linguist and philosopher, dedicated himself to studying the underlying natures of language and the mind. One of the fundamental concepts that developed from his research was that all human language is based on shared principles called _linguistic universals._ One of his universal linguistic rules states that all complete sentences must have both a subject and a predicate. The subject represents the "doer," or "who," of the sentence. The predicate represents the action, or "does what to whom or what." These two components interact with and impact each other in many, sometimes subtle, ways (Chomsky 1957).

In order to understand a Spanish sentence, you must know the linguistic components of which it is comprised and understand how they interact with one another. That means that you can classify sentences by mood or tense and identify the subject, verb, and object(s) of each sentence. If there is a pronoun in the sentence, you must be certain of its antecedent. Do not guess based on a quick glance; _know_ by analyzing the grammatical elements.

Task 1. Complete Chart. Complete the following chart of the relevant parts of speech and their functions for quick reference.

Parts of Speech	Function(s)
Subject:	"Who?"
Noun	
Subject pronoun	
Adjective	
Predicate:	"Does what to whom or what?"
Verb	
Adverb	
Reflexive pronoun	
Direct object	
Direct object pronoun	
Indirect object	
Indirect object pronoun	

Task 2. Define Verbal Elements. In order to unravel a narrative, you need to be able to decode the main verb(s) in any sentence, that is, to separate and clarify the verbal elements based on a key. Define each of the following elements that make up the key for decoding verbs. What information does each element provide?

1. the infinitive: _____

_____

2. the root: _____

_____

3. the person: _____

_____

4. the number: _____

_____

5. the mood: _____

_____

6. the tense: _____

_____

7. the English equivalent: _____

_____

Task 3. Decode Verbs. Decode the underlined verbs in the following passages from *La camisa de Margarita* by completing the chart on the next page. Make sure you can explain your answers.

20   Por supuesto que, mientras le <u>llegaba</u> la ocasión de heredar al tío, vivía nuestro don Luis tan pelado como una rata y pasando la pena negra. Con decir que hasta sus trapicheos <u>eran</u> al fiado y para pagar cuando mejorase de fortuna, creo que <u>digo</u> lo preciso.

En la procesión de Santa Rosa <u>conoció</u> Alcázar a la linda Margarita. La
25   muchacha le llenó el ojo y le flechó el corazón. La echó flores, y aunque ella no le contestó ni sí ni no, <u>dio</u> a entender con sonrisitas y demás armas del arsenal femenino que el galán era plato muy de su gusto. La verdad, como si me <u>estuviera</u> confesando, es que se enamoraron hasta la raíz del pelo.

VERBAL ELEMENTS

Text: _____

VERB	Infinitive	Root	Person	Number	Mood	Tense	English Equivalent
1.							
2.							
3.							
4.							
5.							
6.							

Task 4. Identify Parts of Speech. The following sentences have also been taken from *La camisa de Margarita.* Identify the main parts of speech in each sentence and list them on the following chart.

NOTE: Begin by identifying the verb, or "does what" part, of the predicate. The verb identifies the activity or the state of being that corresponds to the subject. Based on the verb, you can determine the subject, or the "who," and the object, or the "to whom or what," of the sentence. You can also list other grammatical elements that might assist in unraveling the meaning of the sentence, for example, adverbs, adjectives, and *if* clauses.

Margarita Pareja era (por los años de 1765) la hija más mimada de don Raimundo Pareja, caballero de Santiago y colector general del Callao.

La muchacha era una de esas limeñitas que, por su belleza, cautivan al mismo diablo y lo hacen persignarse y tirar piedras. Lucía un par de ojos negros que eran como dos torpedos cargados con dinamita y que hacían explosión sobre las entrete-
15   las del alma de los galanes limeños.

Llegó por entonces de España un arrogante mancebo, hijo de la coronada villa del oso y del madroño, llamado don Luis Alcázar. Tenía éste en Lima un tío solterón y acaudalado, aragonés rancio y linajudo, y que gastaba más orgullo que los hijos del rey Fruela.

PARTS OF SPEECH				
Text:				
Subject	**Verb**	**D.O.**	**I.O.**	**Other**
1.				
2.				
3.				
4.				
5.				

Task 5. Identify Pronouns. In the following paragraphs, identify the type of pronoun, the antecedent of the pronoun, and the grammatical function of the pronoun. To determine the antecedent, trace each pronoun to its source. That is, find the "who and/or what" that the pronoun stands in for.

A don Raimundo no <u>le</u> cayó en gracia la petición; y cortésmente despidió al postulante, diciéndo<u>le</u> que Margarita era aún muy niña para tomar marido, pues, a pesar de sus diez y ocho mayos, todavía jugaba a las muñecas.

35   Pero no era <u>ésta</u> la verdadera madre del ternero. La negativa nacía de que don Raimundo no quería ser suegro de un pobretón; y así hubo de decir<u>lo</u> en confianza a sus amigos, uno de <u>los</u> que fue con el chisme a don Honorato, que así <u>se</u> llamaba el tío aragonés. Este, que era más altivo que el Cid, trino de rabia y dijo:

    —¡Cómo <u>se</u> entiende! ¡Desairar a mi sobrino! Muchos se darían con un canto

40   en el pecho por emparentar con el muchacho, que no <u>le</u> hay más gallardo en todo Lima. ¡Habrá<u>se</u> visto insolencia de la laya! Pero ¿adónde ha de ir con<u>migo</u> ese colectorcito de mala muerte?

PRONOUN IDENTIFICATION

Text: _____

Line No.	Pronoun	Antecedent	Function
_____	_____	_____	_____
_____	_____	_____	_____
_____	_____	_____	_____
_____	_____	_____	_____
_____	_____	_____	_____
_____	_____	_____	_____
_____	_____	_____	_____
_____	_____	_____	_____
_____	_____	_____	_____

Confirm your answers with your study group.

STRATEGY 2. RELATE ACTIONS TO CHARACTERS

Task 1. Complete Graphic Organizer. Expand existing word wheels, or complete the following graphic organizer, with information about the action of the characters. Focus on what the characters do to create the action of the narrative in relationship to themselves, the other characters, and the story itself. Support your information with textual references that include page numbers.

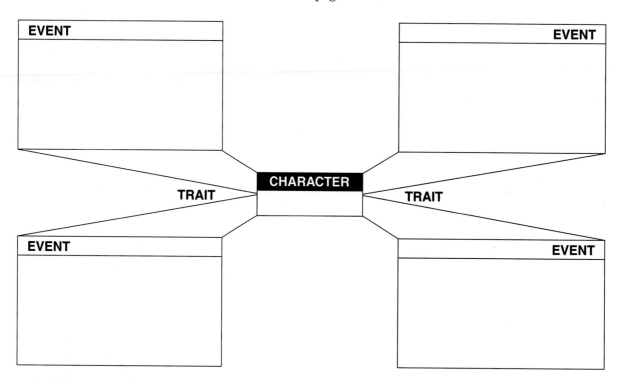

Task 2. Compare and Contrast. Document the relationship between the characters using a venn diagram (see Appendix), indicating their similarities and differences.

STRATEGY 3. SUMMARIZE EACH SEGMENT

Study Hint: Summarizing

A summary is a short version of someone else's ideas written in your own words. It should be composed of several simple statements that are related to your thesis and to each other, and that move the story forward. Simplicity is the key. In order to create an accurate summary, you need to be able to:

- determine the topic sentence of a paragraph;
- invent a topic sentence if there is none;
- delete unnecessary or redundant information;
- substitute a term or event for a list of items or actions; and
- substitute an action word for a list of sub-components of that action.

Task 1. Identify Topic Sentence. A topic sentence states the main point of the paragraph. Although the topic sentence is often the first sentence of the paragraph, it also can be found in the middle or at the end of the paragraph. On your working copy of the text, bracket or underline the topic sentence in each segment. If there is no topic sentence, invent one and write it in the margin next to the segment.

Task 2. Delete Information. Using the same working copy, go from segment to segment and draw a line through redundant information and information that is not central to the theme.

Task 3. Generalize. Look at the information left in the segments. Can it be generalized?

Task 4. Summarize. Based on the information from Tasks 1, 2, and 3, summarize each segment and determine its function in the narrative. Is it a descriptive paragraph, or does it move the text forward? Document your summaries on the numbered sheets you created in Stage II, Strategy 1, Task 2.

STRATEGY 4. CREATE THEMATIC STRUCTURE

Task 1. Identify Thematic Elements. Refer to the chart on **la historia** that you created in **Elementos principales del texto literario** (p. 6). Identify in *La camisa de Margarita* the literary elements defined in that chart. Write the thematic element next to the segment of the text in which it occurs.

Task 2. Complete Thematic Structure. Take all of the information you have gathered so far and use either a sequence chain or a story map (see Appendix) to establish the chain of events in the text. Each "link" in the chain should be an event that moves the story forward. The link may be a change in state of mind, emotion, opinion, or perspective, as well as an event. Substantiate your selections with textual support.

 Compare your work with your study group, then with the other students in your class. Everyone should have ended up with a similar thematic structure. If there are major differences, trace your answers back to their sources and discuss them until you reach a consensus.

Task 3. Ask Yourself. If you are unsure of the answers to these questions, scan the relevant parts of this chapter to refresh your memory.

1. Could you go into your class and discuss all of the narrative elements that you have explored in this chapter?

2. Could you teach another student the strategies you have learned in this chapter?

3. When discussing the narrative in class, will you be able to explain your answers using correct literary terminology?

D. WRITING AND OTHER DIVERSIONS

This section offers a variety of tasks and activities that your instructor can assign, you can do on your own, or you can do with your study group. The more you apply and use your new knowledge, the better you will store it for later retrieval. It is also important to find ways in which you can have fun with your new skills and knowledge.

- Collaboratively create a list of the reading and research strategies that you would feel comfortable using to understand a text. What could you do if you do not understand or if you feel overwhelmed?
- Create an exploratory guide. What questions should be asked in order to determine what happened to whom, where, when, and how? List the kind of textual cues, linguistic cues, and semantic cues that would give you the information you seek.
- Design a structure to explore the thematic construct of a story. Narratives have three general components: the introduction (**la exposición, el desarrollo**), the complication (**el suspenso, el punto decisivo, el clímax**) and the resolution (**el desenlace**). How can the reader identify these different components? What are the lexical cues for each? How do you know when and if the resolution has been reached?
- Write imitative narratives in which the basic story line remains the same but the setting, time, and characters change.
- Re-create the plot within the framework of a current world or national event.

- Write a few paragraphs that imitate the stylistic writing technique of the author.
- Write an alternate ending to the story.
- Select one character and expand upon the character's role in the narrative, as well as his/her relationship with the other characters, using one textual reference as the springboard. (For example, describe the past relationship between two characters that explains their current attitude toward each other.)
- Write yourself into the narrative as an additional character. What is your role in the story and your relationship with the other characters?
- Write about the story as if you were a newspaper reporter.
- Write about the story from the "fly-on-the-wall" perspective in which you know all and see all.

FIGURAS RETÓRICAS

Figuras de pensamiento

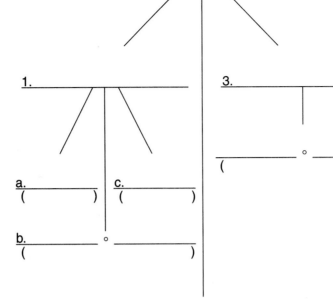

1. _____   3. _____

a. _____   c. _____
(_____)   (_____)

                (_____ ∘ _____)

b. _____ ∘ _____
(_____)

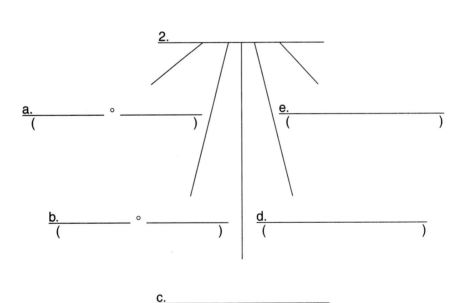

2. _____

a. _____ ∘ _____   e. _____
(_____)   (_____)

b. _____ ∘ _____   d. _____
(_____)   (_____)

c. _____
(_____)

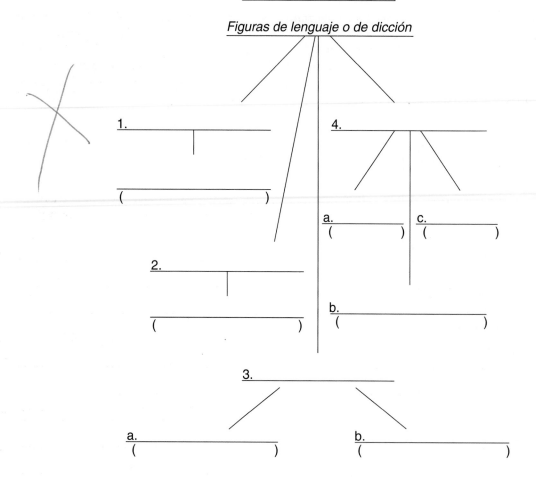

FIGURAS RETÓRICAS

Figuras de lenguaje o de dicción

1. _____
   (_____)

2. _____
   (_____)

3. _____
   a. (_____)   b. (_____)

4. _____
   a. _____
   (_____)   c. _____
   (_____)
   b. _____
   (_____)

2. In what other innate ways might people have used poetry? _____

_____

_____

3. How has poetry's purpose changed since then? _____

_____

_____

Task 2. Identify Key Words. If you were to pursue further research on the origins, purposes, and uses of poetry, what are some key words that would assist in a computer or library search?

_____   _____

_____   _____

_____   _____

NOTE: In the Stages and Strategies section, the sample poem that will be used is *Trinos*, by Ana María Fagundo (p. 216). According to the introduction on page 214, Ana María Fagundo was born in 1938 and is still alive today. She falls into the fundamental category of **la poesía española contemporánea.**

Task 3. Answer Questions. The section entitled **La poesía española contemporánea** on page 141 discusses modern authors of Spain—those who published between 1950 and 1960—as a group. Answer the following questions based on the information in the paragraph.

1. What are the three more popular causes that these poets embraced? _____

_____

2. How did they distinguish themselves from other groups of poets? _____

_____

3. The authors discuss two possible common denominators within the diverse styles of this group of poets. What are these common denominators, and how do they manifest in the poetry?

_____

_____

_____

4. What do the authors consider the most important contribution of the poets like Ana María Fagundo? Why?

_____

_____

_____

D. STAGES AND STRATEGIES
FOR READING POETRY

Objectives:

- To use the Stage I strategies to establish a cultural/historical framework for the poems to be read, in particular *Trinos* by Ana María Fagundo
- To apply the strategies for reading poetry in Stages II, III, and IV to Fagundo's poem

This section will develop the fundamental skills you need to analyze poetry. As you saw in the **Introducción:** Getting Started, all of the literary genres share the first two stages of reading, but the strategies for poetry differ in the third and fourth stages. This has to do with the physical nature of the text. In poetry, every word is critically important, so the reading strategies for poetry must treat each word as a part of the whole.

Remember that the stages and strategies for reading any genre represent a process that builds on itself. With practice, tasks that at first seem awkward or tedious eventually become second nature. Many students find that the ability to analyze poetry is a skill more easily acquired working in groups. What you might not see, someone else will. Therefore, you are strongly encouraged to work with your study group even when not specifically instructed to.

Stage I. Develop Cultural/Historical Framework

STRATEGY 1. CREATE/ADD TO GRAPHIC ORGANIZER

Task 1. Create Graphic Organizer. If you began your study of literature with the narrative, you already should have a cultural/historical framework into which you can insert the information on poetry. If you are beginning with poetry, you will have to create a graphic organizer. For more specific guidelines, see Stage I, Strategy 1, in Chapter 1: **La narrativa** (p. 13).

Task 2. Enter Information. Using your course syllabus, determine the chronological placement of all the poets you will be studying. Enter them into your graphic organizer. As you study these poets and their poetry, you will add the information you discover to your cultural/historical framework, providing yourself with a broad overview of the chronological, cultural, and historical development of Hispanic poetry.

STRATEGY 2. EXPAND BACKGROUND KNOWLEDGE

Task 1. Activate Prior Knowledge. Think about any high school or college class in which you have studied poetry, whether in Spanish or English. What do you remember? Ana María Fagundo wrote after the Spanish Civil War (1936–1939), during the dictatorship of Francisco Franco. What do you know about that historical time in Spain and Europe?

Task 2. Key Word Search. Look at the key words you listed in Task 2 of **Panorama histórico** (p. 51). Now that you know when Ana María Fagundo wrote and published, what words might you add to that list? Use at least three of them within a broader category—for example, geography, language, music—to do a computer and/or library search of that era, relating the information to the poet. Document the key words you use, the category you research, and a brief summary of the information you find.

Key Word			
Category			
Summary			

Task 3. Personal Research. Find a personal source of information (a professor, instructor, local teacher, friend, graduate student, librarian) who is interested in the genre, the poetry and/or history of Spain, the poet, or a related topic. Try to expand your knowledge base by talking to that person about the topic(s) of your research. Document your discoveries here.

1. With whom did you talk? _____

2. What did you learn? _____

_____

_____

_____

_____

_____

3. What could you do to find out more about the topic? _____

_____

_____

_____

STRATEGY 3. USE TEXTBOOK AS RESOURCE

Task 1. Elaborate. Take the information you gathered from the **Panorama histórico** section and Strategy 2, and add it to the graphic organizer from Strategy 1.

Task 2. Skim. Skim **Vida y obra** in the introduction to Ana María Fagundo, on pages 214–215 of the text. How would you describe the quality of her life so far?

_____

_____

_____

Task 3. Scan. Scan **La autora y su contexto** in the introduction to Fagundo. Note the key words and phrases that confirm and/or augment what you learned about her in the **Panorama histórico** section.

_____   _____

_____   _____

_____   _____

Now find at least three additional pieces of information about Fagundo's life or her particular contribution to Spanish poetry—e.g., **la poesía intimista**—and add them to your graphic organizer.

Task 4. Share Information. Combine all of the information about Fagundo that your study group found. What does this tell you about her as a poet?

_____

_____

_____

Stage II. Pre-Reading Observations

Objective:

- To make observations and predictions about the poem based on an examination of its physical and visual cues

Before you begin to read a poem, it is important to study its physical aspects and visual cues—for example, the title, the length of verses and/or stanzas, the punctuation (or lack thereof). These often will give you an idea of what the poem is about. Your goal in this stage is to use your ability to observe, relate, and elaborate. Generate as many ideas as you can; you can determine the relevance of the ideas later. Here quantity, not quality, is the goal.

NOTE: Always keep your cultural/historical framework at hand. All of the poets in *Aproximaciones* were selected for a reason, and part of your job is to determine that reason. Where does the poet being studied fit into the cultural/historical framework and the literary trends of the age? What did his/her style contribute to the genre?

STRATEGY 1. MAKE WORKING COPY OF POEM

It is important for three reasons to have a working copy of the poem you are analyzing. First, some poems have been divided into parts in order to accommodate the space in the text. It is critical to see the poem in its original format so that you can see how the verses and stanzas fit together. Second, you can enlarge your working copy to make the words easier to see. Third, you still have a clean copy of the poem in the text.

Task 1. Create Working Copy. Make a copy of the poem you are studying, in this case *Trinos* on page 216. Cut and paste the copy so that the poem appears as one continuous text, rather than divided. Enlarge the copy as necessary for ease of reading and analysis.

STRATEGY 2. BRAINSTORM ABOUT TITLE

Task 1. Decode Title. Make sure you know exactly what the title means. Look up any words you do not understand. What does the word **trinos** mean?

_____

Task 2. Brainstorm. Review everything you have learned about the poetic style and characteristics of the poet, and brainstorm on all possible meanings of the title. Remember, the title is part of **el lenguaje literario** of the poem. Document your ideas on a word wheel (see Appendix).

STRATEGY 3. SKIM TEXT FOR MAIN IDEA

Task 1. Skim Text. Skim the poem for the gist and write it down. Does the poem focus on a person, a place, an action, an emotion? Think about "who does what to whom or what."

_____

_____

_____

_____

NOTE: If you have difficulty determining the main idea, do the following three tasks.

Task 2. Scan for Nouns. Scan the poem for nouns and determine if they fall into general categories (for instance, people, places, nature, emotions, colors, war, geography, family). Make note of the categories and provide examples of each.

Categories of Nouns	**Examples**
_____	_____
_____	_____
_____	_____

Task 3. Scan for Verbs. Scan the poem for verbs. Separate them into action and state-of-being verbs and write them down. Make note of the subject of each verb you list.

State-of-Being Verbs	**Subject**
_____	_____
_____	_____
_____	_____
_____	_____

Action Verbs	**Subject**
_____	_____
_____	_____
_____	_____
_____	_____

Task 4. Elaborate. Based on the information from Tasks 2 and 3, can you elaborate on your first guess at the main idea of the poem?

_____

_____

_____

STRATEGY 4. BRAINSTORM AND SPECULATE

Task 1. Brainstorm Connections. Arrange in front of you the results of all of the tasks you have done in Stages I and II. Brainstorm possible connections between what you know about the poet and the poem.

Task 2. Speculate. Speculate about the purpose of this poem. Why did the poet write it and what did he/she want the reader to learn, feel, or think? The goal here is not to obtain a correct answer, but rather to think of as many possibilities as you can. You will determine the plausibility later; for now, go ahead and guess.

_____

_____

_____

_____

Share your speculations with your study group.

Task 3. Challenge Yourself. Several passages from the description of Fagundo's style on page 216 of the text are listed here. Find words, expressions, or lines in the poem *Trinos* that might be examples of her style. Add the connections you made in Task 1.

1. "tratar de una manera muy personal la condición humana y los más graves problemas inherentes a ella":

_____

_____

2. "funciona como una ventana al mundo": _____

_____

_____

3. "la poesía representa un universo autónomo": _____

_____

_____

4. "la palabra [representa] una fuente de revelación y conocimiento": _____

_____

_____

Stage III. First Reading

Objective:

- To analyze the versification of the poem

Here you will use all of the strategies you learned and practiced in the first section of this chapter. Refer to that section when necessary. Use your working copy of the poem *Trinos* throughout this stage.

STRATEGY 1. CLASSIFY VERSES

Task 1. Count Poetic Syllables. Follow these steps to determine the number of poetic syllables in each verse.

> **Step 1.** Underline **las sinalefas.**
>
> **Step 2.** Divide the verse into syllables, taking **las sinalefas** into account.
>
> **Step 3.** Write the corresponding numbers above the syllables.
>
> **Step 4.** Determine the classification of the verse and decide if you need to add a syllable (+1), subtract a syllable (–1), or do nothing.
>
> **Step 5.** Write the total number of poetic syllables at the end of the verse.

Task 2. Classify Verses. Determine the classification of each verse based on the number of poetic syllables it contains (refer to the chart on page 39 of this Workbook). Write the classification to the right of the number of syllables on your working copy of the poem.

STRATEGY 2. DETERMINE TYPE AND PATTERN OF RHYME

Task 1. Determine Type of Rhyme. Use the following steps to determine the type of rhyme in the poem.

> **Step 1.** Identify the last word in each verse. Is it **aguda, llana, esdrújula,** or **sobresdrújula**?
>
> **Step 2.** Identify the tonic syllable in each verse-ending word.
>
> **Step 3.** Establish the pattern of sounds. Is the rhyme **asonante, consonante,** or **blanco**?
>
> **Step 4.** Mark the pattern of rhyme on your working copy of the poem. Use lower-case letters, upper-case letters, or the symbol Ø as appropriate. If necessary, consult page 116 of the text.

Task 2. Determine Pattern of Rhyme. Using your working copy of the poem, compare the pattern of rhyme you established with the patterns of rhyme on pages 117–118 of the text. Determine the pattern of rhyme in the poem.

 Compare your results with your study group.

STRATEGY 3. IDENTIFY TYPE OF POEM

Task 1. Determine Type of Stanza. Compare the pattern of rhyme written on your working copy of the poem to the types of stanzas listed on pages 119–120 of the text. If the pattern you identified does not correspond to any of the patterns in the text, double-check your work, then compare your work with your study group. If necessary, ask your instructor. Write the type(s) of stanza on your working copy.

Task 2. Identify Type of Poem. A poem will be **estrófico** or **no estrófico** depending on its pattern of rhyme. Determine what type of poem *Trinos* is, referring to pages 121–122 if necessary. Justify your answer.

Trinos is _____ because _____

_____ .

Task 3. Specify Type of Poem. If it is **un poema estrófico,** it will probably be either **un soneto** or **una letrilla.** If it is **un poema no estrófico,** it will probably be **un romance, una silva,** or **un poema de verso libre.** If the poem does not fall within any of the categories presented in the text, double-check your work, then compare your work with your study group. Finally, ask your instructor. Justify your answer.

Trinos is _____ because _____

_____ .

STRATEGY 4. SCAN EACH SEGMENT FOR INFORMATION

Task 1. Segment Poem. Divide the poem into segments. If it is **un poema estrófico,** draw a line between the stanzas on your working copy. Otherwise, determine another logical way to segment the poem (for example, punctuation or number of verses).

Task 2. Determine the Five W's. Reactivate the information you have documented so far, then scan one segment of the poem at a time. Ascertain the answers to as many of the five W's as you can.

Who? _____

What? _____

Where? _____

When? _____

Why? _____

Task 3. Complete Star Diagram. Organize the answers to the above questions on a star diagram (see Appendix). Each "point" of the star corresponds to one of the five W's. For each point, cite the words or phrases from the text that substantiate your answer. Document all of your observations.

STRATEGY 5. IDENTIFY INFORMATION GAPS

Task 1. Review. Review what you learned about poetry in the first part of this chapter so that you know what it is you need to know in order to understand and discuss this particular literary form.

Task 2. Identify Information Gaps. Make note of the information that you did *not* uncover during Stages II and III. The information that you do not have is just as important as the information that you do. It is fine to not know something at this point, as long as you are aware of what you do know and what you still need to know.

I know: _____

_____

_____

I need to know: _____

_____

_____

Task 3. Identify Vocabulary Gaps. List any words you still do not understand and take the steps necessary to determine their meaning. Remember that at this point you are still working with the direct meaning of the words rather than with their literary or symbolic meaning.

_____

_____

_____

_____

Stage IV. Second Reading

Objective:

- To explore the surface meaning of the poem based on the syntax and literary language, in preparation for analyzing the deeper meaning

The goal of this stage is to create a thematic structure of the poem. To do so you will use all of the skills you developed in the **Introducción a la poesía.** The strategies and tasks in this stage also require you to use the knowledge of syntax that you reviewed in the **Introducción a la narrativa.**

STRATEGY 1. IDENTIFY LITERARY LANGUAGE

Task 1. Review and Scan. Review the classifications of **figuras retóricas** in the graphic organizers you completed in the **Lenguaje literario** section (pp. 47–48). Then scan the poem and identify clear uses of any of these rhetorical figures, making note of them on your working copy. You will revisit them later.

Task 2. Review and Scan. Review the definitions of **tropos** from Task 2 on page 49 in the **Lenguaje literario** section. Then scan the poem again and identify any clear uses of any of these tropes. Make notes on your working copy to refer to later.

 Task 3. Compare. Compare your results from Tasks 1 and 2 with your study group. Discuss your answers.

STRATEGY 2. ANALYZE SYNTAX

Task 1. Rewrite. Use a Parts of Speech chart (see Appendix) to rewrite each sentence or clause in the poem, putting the parts of speech in grammatical order. (Remember that each sentence or clause must contain a subject and a predicate.) The purpose of this task is to confirm that you understand "who does what to whom or what" in the poem.

Task 2. Decode Verbs. Extract the verbs from the poem and write them into a Verbal Elements chart (see Appendix). Decode each verb by determining its verbal elements.

Task 3. Decode Pronouns. Highlight the pronouns in the poem and complete a Pronoun Identification chart (see Appendix) in order to decode the pronouns.

STRATEGY 3. SUMMARIZE EACH SEGMENT

Task 1. Review and Brainstorm. Pull together the results of all the tasks from Strategy 2. Read them and brainstorm about what the poet is trying to say.

Task 2. Summarize. Based on the information in Task 1, summarize each segment of the poem. The summaries can be based on stanzas or on clauses, as long as you include every line.

Task 3. Elaborate. Look at Tasks 1 and 2 in Strategy 1, where you listed the rhetorical figures and tropes in the poem. Reconfirm your first observations, elaborate on them or add others that you did not see, or eliminate those that were incorrect.

STRATEGY 4. CREATE THEMATIC STRUCTURE

Task 1. Complete Graphic Organizer. Use the graphic organizer on the next page, one of the graphic organizers in the Appendix, or one of your own design to document the thematic thread of the poem. This is where you tie together everything you have done in Stage IV.

THEMATIC STRUCTURE

Title of poem: _____

Name of poet: _____

Thematic thread	Literary language

Beginning verses _____

_____   _____

_____   _____

_____   _____

_____   _____

_____   _____

_____   _____

Middle verses _____

_____   _____

_____   _____

_____   _____

_____   _____

_____   _____

_____   _____

End verses _____

_____   _____

_____   _____

_____   _____

_____   _____

NOTE: The last part of this section, in the main text, **Otras formas y técnicas dramáticas,** will be addressed more formally later in this chapter of the Workbook. For now, do the following tasks.

Task 3. Highlight. Using your course syllabus as a guide, scan the sections on pages 231–234 of the text and highlight all of the dramatic selections you are assigned to read. Also highlight one or two phrases that explain the importance or significance of each selection. You will refer to this section again in the Stages and Strategies for Reading Drama.

Task 4. Test Yourself. Before you continue, make sure that you can answer the following questions without referring to your notes.

1. Re-create from memory the graphic organizer you created in Task 4 of **Análisis del teatro.** Then check your answers and fill in any gaps.

2. Define the following terminology to a classmate, being as specific as possible: **el plano textual, el diálogo, los personajes, el espectador, las acotaciones, el plano espectacular.**

   Variation: With your study group, brainstorm definitions for each of these dramatic terms.

3. Working alone or with your study group, draw the diagram that represents **el código comunicativo teatral** and relate the components to the communicative code for the narrative. Remember to include the arrows in your diagram.

4. What is **el proceso dialógico**? (Hint: five levels of communication)

5. Re-create the visual representation of the five levels of communication that make up the **proceso dialógico** in theater that you created in Task 5 of **Plano textual o literario** (p. 69).

6. Explain the differences between **el diálogo directo** and **el diálogo indirecto.**

7. Elaborate on the following formula: *actor + texto = personaje.*

8. What do the authors mean by the statement **"el espectador se integra al espectáculo como un observador participante"**?

9. What is the role of **el texto secundario**?

10. List and define the different components of the textual structure (**la trama**) of a play. What determines where each one begins and ends?

   Task 5. Practice. With your study group, do the **Práctica** section that begins on page 234 of the text. Remember to discuss *how* you determine the answers.

B. PANORAMA HISTÓRICO

Objectives:

- To understand the evolution of drama as a literary form
- To relate each of the dramatists studied to a historical moment and to each other
- To add the dramatists to your cultural/historical framework in order to relate them to writers and poets of the same time periods

EL DRAMA: DEFINICIÓN Y ORÍGENES DEL GÉNERO

Task 1. Skim and Scan. Skim the first paragraph on page 242 of the text. What kind of information does it provide? Scan for answers to the following questions.

1. How do the authors define the word "drama"? _____

_____

_____

2. According to the authors, how does drama differ from narrative and poetry? _____

_____

_____

_____

3. Based on the paragraph, how would you complete this sentence? Drama is

_____ and _____ .

4. Historically speaking, what were the two first dramatic forms?

   a. _____

   b. _____

5. If you were to pursue research on the origins of drama, what are some key words you might use to assist your library or computer search?

_____   _____

_____   _____

_____   _____

NOTE: The sample play for the Stages and Strategies section is *El viejo celoso* by Miguel de Cervantes Saavedra, which begins on page 257 of the text.

Task 2. Read and Answer Questions. The section **El teatro de Miguel de Cervantes** on page 246 briefly presents Cervantes' place in the historical timeline of drama. Read the paragraph and answer the following questions about it.

1. Do you think that Cervantes was a prolific writer? Why or why not? _____

_____

_____

2. Besides drama, to what other genre did Cervantes contribute widely? _____

_____

3. What type of play is *El viejo celoso*? _____

4. Define **un entremés.** _____

_____

_____

5. What does Cervantes strive to communicate through his **entremeses**? _____

_____

_____

6. Based on history and literary movements, what is going on before Cervantes and what happens after Cervantes?

_____

_____

_____

C. STAGES AND STRATEGIES FOR READING DRAMA

Objectives:

- To use the Stage I strategies to elaborate on your cultural/historical framework with information about the plays to be read, in particular *El viejo celoso* by Miguel de Cervantes
- To apply the Stage II, III, and IV strategies for reading drama to Cervantes' play

Reading drama requires an active imagination and the ability to visualize the written word. In theater, what is not said and only seen is just as important as what is said and seen. The language of the play, both verbal and nonverbal, becomes the vehicle for the dramatist's message. As the audience/reader, you play a critical role in the communication of that message. It is your responsibility to read between the lines, to see the shadows in the light, and to give life to the depth and breadth of the characters by knowing more than what is printed on the page. Thus, your exploration of drama must begin with pertinent cultural/historical knowledge.

Stage I. Develop Cultural/Historical Framework

Objective:

- To construct or add to your cultural/historical framework

STRATEGY 1. CREATE/ADD TO GRAPHIC ORGANIZER

Task 1. Create Graphic Organizer. If this is the first genre you study, you will need to create a graphic organizer to serve as your cultural/historical framework. For more specific guidelines, refer to Stage I, Strategy 1, in Chapter 1: **La narrativa** (p. 13).

Task 2. Enter Information. Determine the chronological placement of *El viejo celoso* and enter the information into your graphic organizer.

Task 3. Make Mental Connections. If drama is not the first genre you are studying, there already will be some writers in your cultural/historical framework. Contemplate the structure you have created so far and make note of the historical and chronological relationships between writers in the genres you have studied.

STRATEGY 2. EXPAND BACKGROUND KNOWLEDGE

Task 1. Activate Background Knowledge. Refer back to your answers in Task 1 of **Panorama histórico** (p. 80). Brainstorm examples of "drama" or "theater" you see in your everyday life, on television, or in the classroom. Do you ever find yourself in a position in which you are "performing"? Pick one example and jot down the five W's related to the example.

Example: _____

Who? _____

What? _____

Where? _____

When? _____

Why? _____

How do your examples support Shakespeare's perception that the whole world is a stage?

_____

_____

Task 2. Key Word Search. Use the key words you listed in Task 1 of **Panorama histórico** (p. 80) to do a computer and/or library search within the topic of drama or theater. Document the key words you use, and provide a brief summary of the information you find.

Key Word			
Summary			

Task 3. Expanded Key Word Search. Do a computer and/or library search of the same key words but within a broader, related category (for example, music, art, culture, architecture). What information did you find and how does it relate to the dramatist you are studying, in this case, Cervantes?

Key Word			
Category			
Summary			

Task 4. Personal Research. Find a personal source of information (a professor, instructor, local teacher, friend, graduate student, librarian) who is interested in the genre, the dramatist, the cultural/historical perspective of the epoch in which the dramatist lived and wrote, or a related topic. Try to expand your knowledge base by talking to that person about the topic(s) of your research. Document your discoveries here.

1. With whom did you talk? _____

2. What did you learn? _____

_____

_____

_____

_____

_____

3. What could you do to find out more about the topic? _____

_____

_____

_____

STRATEGY 3. USE TEXTBOOK AS RESOURCE

Task 1. Skim and Scan. Skim **Vida y obra** on page 256 of the text to get a general idea of the quality of Cervantes' life. Was his life difficult or easy? Now scan the same paragraph for answers to the following questions.

1. Was Cervantes' life difficult or easy? _____

2. What are some key words or phrases that indicate the quality of his life?

_____   _____

_____   _____

3. How often was Cervantes imprisoned? _____

4. Did Cervantes die rich or poor? How do you know the answer? _____

_____

_____

5. How might the quality of Cervantes' life have influenced his writing? What kind of attitude, sense of humor, opinions, perspectives, and so forth, might you expect?

_____

_____

_____

_____

Task 2. Skim and Scan. Skim the second part of the introduction to Cervantes, **El autor y su contexto,** and comment on how Cervantes' quality of life affected him as a writer. Then scan the same paragraph to determine the answers to the following questions.

1. How did the quality of Cervantes' life affect him as a writer? _____

_____

_____

2. Where did Cervantes find his inspiration? _____

_____

_____

3. The authors list four characteristics of Cervantes' style that make his literary contribution **"una joya de las letras de todos los tiempos."** What are those stylistic characteristics?

    • _____

    • _____

    • _____

    • _____

4. What do the authors say specifically about *El viejo celoso*? _____

_____

_____

5. Define the origin and meaning of the word "cuckold." _____

_____

_____

Stage II. Pre-Reading Observations

Objective:

- To make observations and predictions about the play using words and phrases as clues to meaning

Your goal in Stage II is to engage your mind actively by searching the literary text for physical and visual clues that will establish the purpose for reading it and will help you predict its meaning. Using these clues and your own background knowledge, you will explore the text and speculate on what you might learn from it. Certain words and phrases will suggest a context, which may or may not be correct, and the context in turn will trigger information about similar situations you may have experienced, read about, or heard about. The results of your pre-reading observations will then provide the basis for free association exercises. Stay open to all possibilities. Here quantity of thought is the goal; correctness of thought can be determined later.

STRATEGY 1. MAKE WORKING COPY OF TEXT

Task 1. Copy Text. Photocopy the play from the textbook. Use this copy for all of your work so that later you can go back to the textbook and read the play without any notes.

Task 2. Segment Text. There are 371 lines in the play. If you make each segment approximately 25 lines long, there will be about 15 segments.

Task 3. Number Segments. Number the segments and write those numbers on a separate sheet of paper. Remember to allow plenty of space to write about each segment; if possible, have no more than two segments per page. You will use this numbered paper to document observations and information about the corresponding segments.

STRATEGY 2. BRAINSTORM ABOUT TITLE

Task 1. Review. Look back at Task 2 in Stage I, Strategy 3, and review the origin and definition of a "cuckold." Also review the information about Cervantes' attitude toward society.

Task 2. Brainstorm. Based on the information from Task 1, brainstorm about *El viejo celoso*. What might the play be about? Will it be satirical or realistic? Who might do what to whom?

 Share your ideas with your study group.

STRATEGY 3. SKIM TEXT FOR MAIN IDEA

Task 1. Skim Each Segment. Working through one segment at a time, skim for the main idea. Make notes on the numbered paper you created to correspond with the segments. Make note of characters' names and the gist of the action. Write one or two sentences for each segment. Be sure to make note of the relevant lines in the text so that you can substantiate your observations.

STRATEGY 4. BRAINSTORM AND SPECULATE

 Task 1. Compare. Compare observations from Strategy 3 with the members of your study group. Make sure everyone provides textual support to substantiate the observations.

Task 2. Elaborate. Elaborate on your own answers with the information provided by your study group.

Task 3. Brainstorm and Speculate. Brainstorm about the main idea of the play. Fill in any gaps that exist after completing Tasks 1 and 2. Speculate on why the action takes place and how the action might affect the outcome of the play.

 Share your results with your study group.

Stage III. First Reading

Objective:

- To scan for specific grammatical and textual elements that provide basic information about the play

This stage relies on recognition of linguistic elements to foster the first level of comprehension of the text. This is the fact-finding stage. It is important to keep your information well organized.

STRATEGY 1. ANALYZE FIRST AND FINAL SEGMENTS

Task 1. Analyze First Segment. Use a fact sheet (see Appendix) to analyze the first segment of the play. Record the verb tenses used, the type of vocabulary, and any other information that may be important.

Task 2. Analyze Final Segment. Use another fact sheet to analyze the final segment. Record the verb tenses used, examples of the vocabulary, and any other general information that might be important.

Task 3. Speculate. Look back at the results of Task 1. How does the first segment relate to the title of the play? What kind of tone does it set? What kind of information does it offer? Next do the same with the results of Task 2. Finally, compare the first segment to the final segment. How do they relate or not relate to each other? What kind of closure does the final segment offer, or not offer?

_____

_____

_____

_____

_____

_____

 Share your speculations with your study group.

STRATEGY 2. SCAN EACH SEGMENT FOR INFORMATION

Task 1. Highlight Stage Directions. Scan the play, segment by segment, and highlight all of the stage directions, which are written in italics.

Task 2. Skim and Scan. Using your segmented working copy of the text and blank fact sheets, work through the remaining segments of the play. First, skim for information to expand the main ideas, then scan for specific verbs that reflect the main action. Record all of your observations. Remember, each time you look at the text you will see more.

 Task 3. Compare. With your study group, compare the results of the first two tasks and fill in any gaps that exist in your individual analyses.

STRATEGY 3. CREATE WORD WHEEL FOR EACH CHARACTER

Task 1. Create Word Wheels. Based on all of the work you have done so far, you should already have extracted the characters' names and determined a rough idea of their role in the play. Create a word wheel for each character that describes what each one is like. Make sure you can support your descriptions with textual references.

Task 2. Compare. Compare your results from Task 1 with your study group. Clarify and/or elaborate when appropriate.

STRATEGY 4. COMPLETE STAR DIAGRAM WITH ANSWERS TO THE "FIVE W'S"

Task 1. Scan for Information. Scan the play and mark the words or phrases that answer the following questions.

> **Who?** The teller (**el dramaturgo / el actor / el narrador**) and the hearer (**el receptor / el espectador**) of the play
>
> **What?** What happens to whom (**la trama**)
>
> **Where?** The historical and/or geographical context or space of the play (**la exposición**)
>
> **When?** The time frame of the play (**el espacio escénico**)
>
> **Why?** The purpose or meaning of the play (**el mensaje del texto dramático**)

Task 2. Create Star Diagram. Organize the answers from Task 1 on a star diagram (see Appendix). For each "point," cite the words or phrases from the text that substantiate your answer. Remember that the more observations you document, the more likely you will be to perceive patterns, redundancies, and dominant images.

STRATEGY 5. IDENTIFY INFORMATION GAPS

Task 1. Review. Review what you learned about the theater in the first part of this chapter so that you know what it is you need to know in order to understand and discuss this particular literary form.

Task 2. Identify Information Gaps. Make note of the information that you did *not* uncover during Stages II and III. The information that you do not have is just as important as the information that you do. It is fine to not know something at this point, as long as you are aware of what you do know and what you still need to know.

I know: _____

_____

_____

I need to know: _____

_____

_____

Task 3. Identify Vocabulary Gaps. List any vocabulary or concept that you do not understand. It is important to begin by trying to clarify confusion on your own. Try to guess at meaning based on root words, context, and prior knowledge about story formats and similar situations. Then consult the textbook, a dictionary, and/or another classmate. Finally, ask your instructor. Write down what you learn about each vocabulary item or concept.

_____

_____

_____

_____

Stage IV. Second Reading

Objective:

- To create a thematic structure of the play

With your pre-reading observations and the information from the first reading, your task here is to determine *what happens to whom* by breaking the text down into parts and putting the parts back together in a way that makes sense to you. You create this thematic structure through a thorough exploration of the text's surface structure, or syntax.

STRATEGY 1. REVIEW RELEVANT SYNTAX

Task 1. Review Stage Directions. Skim through the text and re-read all of the stage directions in order to reactivate your understanding of the basic unspoken action and interaction of the actors. Make sure you understand the stage directions.

Task 2. Transfer and Paraphrase. Transfer the stage directions to the numbered pages that correspond to your segmented working copy of the text. This way you will know when in the text the specific stage directions occur. As you transfer the directions, paraphrase them so that you understand clearly what the actors are doing.

Task 3. Decode Verbs. In Stage III, Strategies 1 and 2, you identified the verbs that create the action of the play. Decode those verbs so that you know who does what to whom, and record the information on a Verbal Elements chart (see Appendix).

Task 4. Identify and Decode Pronouns. Scan the segments and identify critical pronouns. Decode them and record the information on a Pronoun Identification chart (see Appendix). Make sure that you can identify the antecedent of each pronoun.

Task 5. Decode Sentences. If you are not completely clear on "who does what to whom or what," decode the sentences that contain the verbs and pronouns you decoded in Tasks 3 and 4. Use a Parts of Speech chart (see Appendix) to record the information.

STRATEGY 2. RELATE ACTIONS TO CHARACTERS

Task 1. Complete Word Wheels. Expand your existing word wheel for each character or fill in a character/event diagram (see Appendix) with information that relates actions to characters. Focus on what the characters do to create the action of the play in relationship to themselves, to other characters, and to the story itself. Support your information with textual references that include page numbers.

Task 2. Compare and Contrast. Use a venn diagram (see Appendix) to document relationships between characters, indicating their similarities and differences.

Study Hint: Dramatic Representation

Now is a good time to practice what the authors of *Aproximaciones* call **"la representación dramática."** Although this aspect of theater is not formally addressed in the text, it is through the dramatic representation or performance of a play that the dramatist ultimately delivers the true message. Based on the work you have done so far, select a segment or scene that either appealed to you or that gave you some trouble, and read it out loud. While reading, think about the poetic elements you studied in Chapter 2: **La poesía,** including rhyme, rhythm, accentuation, and intonation. Project yourself into the character(s) in the play based on what you know about the author as well. Which words or phrases should be emphasized? Are there written and/or implied stage directions to which you need to respond? How might they affect your reading? Can you relate other dramatic components to the segment? If you were a director, how might you stage the scene? Try to breathe the kind of life into **el plano espectacular** that cannot be created when you work solely with the words of the play. Take risks! Have fun!

STRATEGY 3. SUMMARIZE EACH SEGMENT

Task 1. Identify Topic Sentence. Using your working copy of the play, bracket or underline the topic sentence(s) of each segment. If there is no clear topic sentence, invent one and write it in the margin next to the segment.

Task 2. Delete Information. Skim your working copy, segment by segment, and draw a line through redundant information or information that is not central to the action of the play.

Task 3. Generalize. Look at the information left in the segments. Can it be generalized?

Task 4. Summarize. Based on the information from Tasks 1, 2, and 3, summarize each segment and determine its function in the play. Is it a descriptive paragraph, does it just provide information, or does it move the action of the play forward?

STRATEGY 4. CREATE THEMATIC STRUCTURE

Task 1. Identify Thematic Elements. Using the chart from Task 2 of **Estructura de la obra dramática** (p. 78) as a guide, identify in the text the components of the dramatic action in the play (**la exposición, el incidente o la complicación, el nudo o clímax,** and **el desenlace**). Write each component next to the segment in which it occurs.

Task 2. Complete Thematic Structure. Take all of the information you have gathered so far and use a story map (see Appendix) to set up the chain of events in the text. Each event in the story map should move the story toward the solution. The event may be a change in state of mind, emotion, opinion, or perspective, as well as a situation or an action. Substantiate your selections with textual support.

 Task 3. Compare. Compare your results from Task 2 with your study group or other students in your class. Everyone should have ended up with a similar thematic structure. If there are any major differences, trace your answers back to their textual sources, discuss them with your classmates, and determine the more correct answer.

NOTE: Upon completing the four stages, you have fulfilled your responsibility as the reader of the play. You know who did what to whom, why, and when. You can talk about the communicative code and the roles of the dramatist, the performer, the dialogue, the scene and stage directions, and the spectator. At this point you are ready to go to class and enter into a well-informed discussion of the play.

D. WRITING AND OTHER DIVERSIONS

This section offers a variety of tasks and activities that your instructor can assign, you can do on your own, or you can do with your study group. The more you apply and use your new knowledge, the better you will store it for later retrieval. It is also important to find ways in which you can have fun with your new skills and knowledge.

- Work with your study group to create an exploratory guide for drama. What are some clues and cues to watch for in the play? What are the critical questions to ask in order to complete the stages and strategies developed in this Workbook? Which strategies worked and which did not work for you?
- Write yourself into the play as a character. Describe your relationship with the characters and your contribution to the action.
- Rewrite the play in a contemporary setting.
- Comment on the play from the perspective of an outside observer, the "fly on the wall" point of view.
- Expand the relationship between two of the characters. Provide the history or background of that relationship that is not provided in the play itself.
- Design a quilt (**un guadamecí**) and describe its role and significance in the play.

- Rewrite the last scene to give the play an alternate ending.
- Depict the characters as they might appear on a talk show about infidelity or impotence. What would they say? How would they act?
- Interview one or two of the characters. What would you ask them and what might they answer?
  - Form groups, select a scene from the play, and produce it. Design the set and costumes and explain how the actors will deliver the lines. Perform the scene for your class.

- Write your own **entremés,** either individually or with your study group, maintaining all of the "flavor" that was typical of the dramatic format.

CHAPTER 4

EL ENSAYO

Objective:

- To establish the knowledge base and reading skills necessary for understanding and discussing the essay, by
  - exploring the **Introducción al ensayo** on pages 336–343 of the main text
  - examining the characteristics of different types of essays
  - applying the Stage I strategies to add information on the sample essay, *Y las madres, ¿qué opinan?* by Rosario Castellanos, to your cultural/historical framework
  - implementing the Stage II, III, and IV strategies as they apply to the sample essay in order to develop the skills necessary for reading essays with comprehension

The essay is a relatively short literary composition, with the most flexible structure and style of the four major literary genres, which makes it a very popular format for writing. There are many different kinds of essays, each with a unique combination of characteristics that ultimately draw on all the other literary forms. Essays can be directed to the mass audience or to a specific group of readers and can vary in degree of awareness (or lack of awareness) of the audience. In his book *The Art of Interpretation* (Bacon & Breene, 1961), Wallace Bacon writes that, "rather than creating a world of its own, as the literary work does, [the essay] tends to join the reader in the actual world to talk about something in which narrator and reader have a common interest—to create one side of a dialogue in which the reader supplies the other half" (412). The participation of the reader is more direct than in other literary genres, and the reader functions more as the recipient of the message rather than as the interpreter. Your response as the reader becomes the focus of the essayist's purpose for writing.

A. INTRODUCCIÓN AL ENSAYO

Objectives:

- To break the information presented in the **Introducción al ensayo** (pp. 335–361) into manageable sections and extract the most pertinent information from those sections
- To develop the background knowledge and language necessary to understand and discuss the formats and purposes of the essay as a literary form

I. El ensayo como género literario

Task 1. Scan for Information. Scan the first paragraph of the introduction, on page 336 of the text, for answers to the following questions.

1. According to the authors, what role does literature in general play in the human existence? ___

_____

_____

_____

2. What specific role does the essay fulfill? _____

_____

_____

3. List three specific examples of "essays" that you see in your daily life. _____

_____

_____

_____

 Task 2. Differentiate. Scan the second paragraph on page 336 for the fundamental way in which the essay differs from the narrative, poetry, and drama.

_____

_____

_____

What key word could you use to pinpoint the difference? _____

 Task 3. Paraphrase. In the third paragraph on page 336, the authors state that, within the genre, there are two general kinds of essays. Read and then paraphrase the definitions the authors present.

1. _____

_____

2. _____

_____

Task 4. Brainstorm. Brainstorm about the possible characteristics of each kind of essay you defined in Task 3. If you already have explored the other literary genres, activate what you know about them in order to trigger your brainstorm.

1. _____

_____

_____

2. _____

_____

_____

II. El ensayo: definición y categorías fundamentales

 Task 1. Scan and Paraphrase. The first paragraph of this section, on page 336, offers an extensive definition of the essay based on three aspects: language, purpose, and point of view. Scan the paragraph for information that explains the role of each aspect in defining the essay, and paraphrase that information on the following page.

1. Language: ———————————————————————————————————

   ———————————————————————————————————

   ———————————————————————————————————

2. Purpose: ———————————————————————————————————

   ———————————————————————————————————

   ———————————————————————————————————

3. Point of view: ———————————————————————————————

   ———————————————————————————————————

   ———————————————————————————————————

According to the last sentence of the same paragraph, what important variable does the essay share with the narrative, poetry, and drama?

———————————————————————————————————

———————————————————————————————————

Task 2. Define. In the same paragraph that you read for Task 1, find the word *Zeitgeist* and define it.

Zeitgeist: ———————————————————————————————

———————————————————————————————————

———————————————————————————————————

What are several *Zeitgeist* that you would relate to your particular generation?

1. ———————————————————————————————

2. ———————————————————————————————

3. ———————————————————————————————

4. ———————————————————————————————

EL ENSAYO EN RELACIÓN CON LAS DEMÁS FORMAS LITERARIAS

Task 1. Brainstorm. Look at the continuum at the top of page 337. Without reading the accompanying text, use what you have learned so far to brainstorm reasons why each genre is placed where it is on the continuum in relation to the others.

———————————————————————————————————

———————————————————————————————————

———————————————————————————————————

———————————————————————————————————

Task 2. Read and Compare. Now read the paragraph that explains the continuum and compare your reasons to the statements in the paragraph. What is the variable shared by the different genres that determines their position on the continuum?

_____

_____

_____

Task 3. Complete. Based on the information from Tasks 1 and 2, fill in the continuum with the fundamental differences between the four genres.

| ensayo | obra narrativa | pieza teatral | poema |

Task 4. Explain. Explain to your study group why and how the four genres are connected, and why and how they are separate.

EL ENSAYO: SU CLASIFICACIÓN

Task 1. Define. Based on the first paragraph of this section, on page 337 of the text, define the four classifications of essay presented by the authors. Give an example in either English or Spanish of each type of essay.

1. el ensayo poético: _____

    _____

    _____

    Example: _____

2. el ensayo dramático: _____

    _____

    _____

    Example: _____

3. el ensayo narrativo: _____

    _____

    _____

    Example: _____

4. el ensayo ensayístico: _____

    _____

    _____

    Example: _____

Task 2. Identify Key Words. Select a key word or words from each definition that will help you remember the differences between the essay types.

TYPE OF ESSAY   KEY WORD(S)

el ensayo poético   _____

_____

el ensayo dramático   _____

_____

el ensayo narrativo   _____

_____

el ensayo ensayístico   _____

_____

Task 3. Scan for Information. Scan the last paragraph on page 337 of the text for answers to the following questions.

1. What is the final goal of every essay, no matter the classification? _____

_____

2. Justify your answer to the first question with textual support. _____

_____

_____

_____

3. What determines the point of view or perspective of which the essayist strives to convince the reader?

_____

_____

_____

4. In the last two sentences of the paragraph, the authors point out important characteristics of the methods of persuasion used by the essayist in **un ensayo persuasivo,** versus the essayist's methods in an essay based on drama, narrative, or poetry. What are the characteristics of these two methods?

a. With **el ensayo persuasivo** the method is _____ and _____ .

b. With essays based on drama, narrative, and poetry the methods are _____

or _____ .

Task 4. Study and Re-Create. The diagram on page 338 of the text represents the ways in which an essayist can formulate the persuasive structure of the essay based on the characteristics of the other genres. Study the diagram, review the work you did in Tasks 1 and 2, and make sure you understand how the diagram represents the relationships between the genres. Then close your text and complete the diagram from memory on the following page.

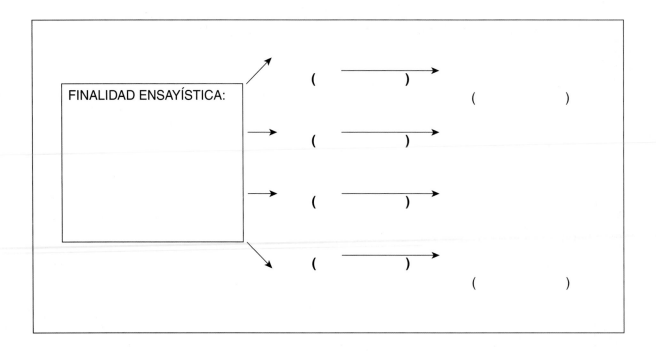

FINALIDAD ENSAYÍSTICA:

(   )

(   )

(   )

(   )

(   )

(   )

 Task 5. Explain. Explain to your study group or another classmate the relationship that the essay has with the other three genres presented in *Aproximaciones*.

Task 6. Challenge Yourself. In the square below, design another diagram or graphic organizer that represents the same information presented in the diagram on page 338.

Share your redesign with your study group. Do they understand it?

Task 7. Brainstorm. With your study group, brainstorm in Spanish about the language (for example, verb tenses, word choices, etc.) that the essayist might use to accomplish the purpose of each type of essay. Document the results of your brainstorm on a graphic organizer such as a word wheel (see Appendix).

III. La oratoria como ensayo: sus características

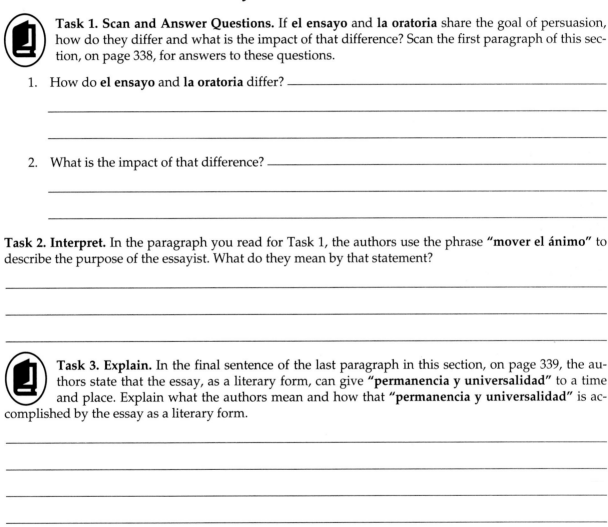

Task 1. Scan and Answer Questions. If **el ensayo** and **la oratoria** share the goal of persuasion, how do they differ and what is the impact of that difference? Scan the first paragraph of this section, on page 338, for answers to these questions.

1. How do **el ensayo** and **la oratoria** differ? _____

_____

_____

2. What is the impact of that difference? _____

_____

_____

Task 2. Interpret. In the paragraph you read for Task 1, the authors use the phrase **"mover el ánimo"** to describe the purpose of the essayist. What do they mean by that statement?

_____

_____

_____

Task 3. Explain. In the final sentence of the last paragraph in this section, on page 339, the authors state that the essay, as a literary form, can give **"permanencia y universalidad"** to a time and place. Explain what the authors mean and how that **"permanencia y universalidad"** is accomplished by the essay as a literary form.

_____

_____

_____

_____

_____

 Task 4. Scan for Textual Support. Scan all of the paragraphs you have read so far in this chapter and find textual support for the explanations you offered in Tasks 2 and 3. Enter the statements and the textual support (including page, paragraph, and sentence numbers) in the chart on the following page.

Statement	Textual Support
"mover el ánimo"	
• _____ _____ _____	_____ _____
• _____ _____ _____	_____ _____
• _____ _____ _____	_____ _____
• _____ _____	_____ _____
"permanencia y universalidad"	
• _____ _____ _____	_____ _____
• _____ _____ _____	_____ _____
• _____ _____ _____	_____ _____
• _____ _____	_____ _____

Task 5. Compare and Create Summary. Compare your chart with your study group. As a group, select the best-supported statements and create a summary of the essay as a literary form to share with the rest of the class.

Task 6. Discuss. Discuss the following question with your study group: Could the concept of **"permanencia y universalidad"** and the phrase **"mover el ánimo"** be applied to the other literary genres you have studied (narrative, poetry, and drama)? Justify your statements with textual support.

IV. Estrategias de persuasión: la lógica formal y la lógica informal

Task 1. Create Word Wheel. According to the authors, there are two strategic formats that essayists can use to persuade their readers. Read the first paragraph of this section on page 339 of the text and determine the two formats. Create a word wheel (see Appendix) for each format and fill in the information presented in the paragraph.

Task 2. Add to Word Wheel. Begin with the word wheel for **la exposición.** Scan the next two paragraphs in this section for information on **la exposición** and add that information to your word wheel.

Task 3. Summarize. Briefly summarize what you have discovered about **la exposición** as a persuasive strategy. What are some examples of the expository format?

Summary: _____

_____

_____

Examples: _____

_____

_____

Task 4. Add to Word Wheel. Now work with the word wheel for **el argumento.** Extract information on **el argumento** as a persuasive strategy from the next paragraph in this section, on page 340 of the text, and add that information to your word wheel.

Task 5. Summarize. Briefly summarize what you have learned about **el argumento** as a persuasive strategy. What are some examples of the argumentative format?

Summary: _____

_____

_____

Examples: _____

_____

_____

Task 6. Scan and Elaborate. Scan the second full paragraph on page 340 for any additional information on either **la exposición** or **el argumento** that you can add to your word wheels. Elaborate on your summary of each format with the new information.

Task 7. Define. The following terms represent strategic approaches that essayists can use to formulate their argument. Based on your work in the previous tasks, you should be able to define the terms without referring to your notes. First define them from memory, then consult your notes to confirm and elaborate on each definition.

1. la hipótesis o las premisas: _____

_____

_____

2. los razonamientos o las proposiciones: _____

_____

_____

3. la tesis o la conclusión: _____

_____

_____

4. los teoremas: _____

_____

_____

5. los axiomas: _____

_____

_____

Task 8. Explain. What do the authors mean by the last sentence in the paragraph you read in Task 6? What does it imply for the reader of the essay? **"Sin embargo, en los mejores ensayos el hábil autor no vacila en emplear armoniosamente exposición y argumento, así como cualquier otro recurso no literario... "**

_____

_____

_____

_____

_____

_____

Task 9. Compare. The chart on page 340 of the text lists examples of expository and argumentative formats. Compare that list to your examples of **la exposición** from Task 3 and **el argumento** from Task 5. Note which ones you included and which ones you overlooked, and add the formats you overlooked to your list of examples.

V. Diferentes tipos de ensayo

Task 1. Scan and Highlight. In this section, on pages 340–342, the authors present four different types of essay. Scan the description of each type and highlight its major characteristics and functions.

Task 2. Complete Graphic Organizer. Transfer the highlighted information from Task 1 to word wheels or another graphic organizer that works for you. Use one graphic organizer for each type of essay.

Task 3. Compare and Elaborate. Compare your completed word wheels or graphic organizers with your study group. Share your findings and add pertinent information.

Task 4. Determine Key Characteristics. With your study group, determine the key characteristic of each type of essay that will help you recognize and differentiate between the types. What will you look for in the essay? Complete the chart on the next page.

Type of Essay	Key characteristic

VI. El ensayo en la actualidad

Task 1. Scan. Here the authors put forth several perspectives of the role of the essay in today's reality. Scan the paragraph on page 343 for answers to the following questions.

1. What does Julio César López González say about the essay? _____
_____
_____

2. According to the authors, the novel is the most popular literary form and the essay is the second most popular. To what do they attribute the essay's popularity?
_____
_____
_____

3. What does Oscar Sambrano Urdaneta add to the discussion? _____
_____
_____

4. In the last sentence of this paragraph, the authors include you, the reader, when they refer to **los jóvenes de hoy.** What do they say about **los jóvenes de hoy**?
_____
_____
_____

5. Do you agree with what they say and do you include yourself in that group? Explain your answer.

_____

_____

_____

Task 2. Test Yourself. Before you continue, make sure that you can answer the following questions without referring to your notes.

1. How does the essay differ from the narrative, poetry, and drama?

2. Within **el género ensayístico** there are two general types of composition. What are they and how would you describe them?

3. The essay establishes its uniqueness through three characteristics: language, purpose, and point of view. Define each of these characteristics.

4. What is *Zeitgeist*? Give several examples.

5. What are the four classifications of essay presented by the authors, and what are some of the key differences between these classifications?

6. What do the authors mean by the following statements?

   • **"El ensayo tiene el propósito de mover el ánimo de los lectores."**
   • **"Por la forma literaria del ensayo, el momento y el lugar adquieren permanencia y universalidad."**

7. An essayist can present his or her persuasive message in two forms: **la exposición** and **el argumento.** Define each form based on its key characteristics and functions.

8. Fill in the following diagram without referring to your notes.

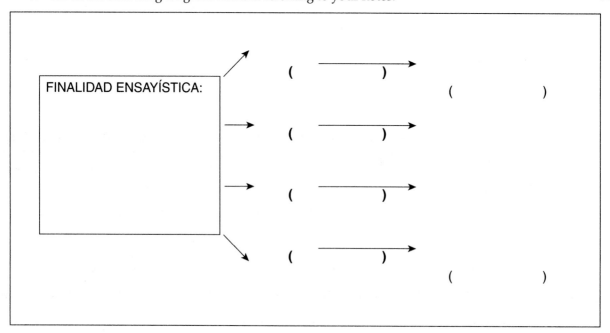

Task 3. Practice. Work through the **Práctica** section on pages 343–346 with a classmate or your study group. Be sure to discuss how you determine the answers.

B. PANORAMA HISTÓRICO

Objectives:

- To understand the evolution of the essay as a literary form
- To relate each of the essayists you study to a historical event and to each other

EL ENSAYO: ORÍGENES, ETIMOLOGÍA, EVOLUCIÓN
Y OBJETIVOS

 Task 1. Skim and Scan. Skim the first paragraph of this section, on page 346 of the text, to determine what kind of information it offers. Then scan the paragraph for answers to the following questions.

1. What kind of information does this paragraph offer about the essay as a literary form?

_____

_____

_____

2. What is the origin of the word **ensayo**? _____

_____

_____

3. According to the authors, what was the original purpose of the essay? _____

_____

_____

NOTE: Remember that the sample essay for this chapter is *Y las madres, ¿qué opinan?* by Rosario Castellanos.

 Task 2. Scan and Answer Questions. The segment **La actualidad: individualismo y reivindicación** on page 358 includes Rosario Castellanos in the most recent group of essayists who have sustained and promoted civil duties and activism by writing about their political, social, and personal views. Scan the paragraph for answers to the following questions.

1. What stylistic tendencies figure prominently in the essays of this group of writers? _____

_____

_____

2. The authors describe the role of Rosario Castellanos and other contemporary female writers as

   "el papel de _____ **e** _____ **."**

3. How do you think these characteristics might be expressed in their essays? _____

_____

_____

_____

4. Name several other contemporary female writers mentioned by the authors. _____

_____

_____

_____

5. What literary techniques do these writers use to promote civil duties and activism? _____

_____

_____

6. If you were to do more research on this group of essayists, what are some key words you might use to assist your computer or library search?

_____   _____

_____   _____

_____   _____

C. STAGES AND STRATEGIES FOR READING ESSAYS

Objectives:

- To use the Stage I strategies to elaborate on your cultural/historical framework with information about the essays to be read, in particular *Y las madres, ¿qué opinan?* by Rosario Castellanos
- To apply the strategies for reading essays in Stages II, III, and IV to Castellanos' work

Stage I. Develop Cultural/Historical Framework

Objective:

- To construct or add to your cultural/historical framework

STRATEGY 1. CREATE/ADD TO GRAPHIC ORGANIZER

Task 1. Create Graphic Organizer. If this is the first genre you study, you will need to create a graphic organizer to serve as your cultural/historical framework. For more specific guidelines, refer to Stage I, Strategy 1, in Chapter 1: **La narrativa** (p. 13).

Task 2. Enter Information. Determine the chronological placement of Rosario Castellanos and enter her into your graphic organizer.

Task 3. Make Mental Connections. Make note of any writers, poets, and dramatists you have studied already and their relationship to Rosario Castellanos. Are there any similarities in their styles or in the topics they write about? What are the differences?

Similarities: _____

_____

_____

Differences: _____

_____

_____

STRATEGY 2. EXPAND BACKGROUND KNOWLEDGE

Task 1. Activate Background Knowledge. Go back to the first task in the **Introducción al ensayo** where you answered questions about the role of the essay and listed examples of essays from your daily life (pp. 91–92). Brainstorm answers to the five W's related to at least one of your examples.

Example: _____

Who? _____

What? _____

Where? _____

When? _____

Why? _____

Is there a pattern of information that might be applied to your other examples, or to essays in general? Are there common characteristics that all essays share? What are they?

_____

_____

_____

Task 2. Key Word Search. Refer back to the key words you listed in Task 2 of **Panorama histórico** (p. 104). Select one key word and use it to do a computer and/or library search. Document the key words you use, and provide a brief summary of the information you find.

Key Word			
Summary			

Task 3. Expanded Key Word Search. Do a computer and/or library search of the same key words but within a broader, related category (for example, music, art, culture, anthropology, architecture). What information did you find and how does it relate to the essayist you are studying, in this case, Castellanos?

Key Word			
Category			
Summary			

Task 4. Personal Research. Find a personal source of information (a professor, instructor, local teacher, friend, graduate student, librarian) who is interested in the genre, the essayist, the topic, or the cultural/historical perspective of the epoch in which the essayist lived and wrote. Try to expand your knowledge base by talking to that person about the topic(s) of your research. Document your discoveries here.

1. With whom did you talk? _____

2. What did you learn? _____

_____

_____

_____

_____

_____

3. What could you do to find out more about the topic? _____

_____

_____

_____

STRATEGY 3. USE TEXTBOOK AS RESOURCE

Task 1. Skim and Scan. Skim **Vida y obra** in the introduction to Rosario Castellanos (p. 380). What kind of information does it provide? Scan the paragraph for answers to the following questions.

1. What kind of information does this paragraph provide? _____

   _____

   _____

2. Rosario Castellanos was a prolific writer. Name the different literary formats in which she wrote and published.

   _____

   _____

3. What are the characteristics and/or themes that dominate Castellanos' writing? _____

   _____

   _____

   _____

Task 2. Skim and Scan. Skim the second part of the introduction to Castellanos, **La autora y su contexto.** What kind of information does it offer? Scan the paragraph to answer the following questions.

1. What kind of information does this paragraph offer? _____

   _____

   _____

2. What early event probably impacted the life and writing of Rosario Castellanos? _____

   _____

   _____

3. What social cause did Castellanos embrace early in her life, and how did that cause manifest in the thematic focus of her works?

   _____

   _____

   _____

4. Specifically concerning the essay **Y las madres, ¿qué opinan?**, what do the authors of *Aproximaciones* say?

   _____

   _____

   _____

5. Based on what you know so far about Rosarios Castellanos, what might be some characteristics of her writing style? Why do you think so?

_____

_____

_____

Stage II. Pre-Reading Observations

Objective:

- To make observations and predictions about the essay using words and phrases as clues to meaning

Your goal in Stage II is to engage your mind actively by searching the literary text for physical and visual clues that will establish the purpose for reading it and will help you predict its meaning. Using these clues and your own background knowledge, you will explore the text and speculate on what you might learn from it. Certain words and phrases will suggest a context, which may or may not be correct, and the context in turn will trigger information about similar situations you may have experienced, read about, or heard about. The results of your pre-reading observations will then provide the basis for free association exercises. Stay open to all possibilities. Here quantity of thought is the goal; correctness of thought can be determined later.

STRATEGY 1. MAKE WORKING COPY OF TEXT

Task 1. Copy Text. Photocopy the essay from the textbook. Use this copy for all of your work so that later you can go back to the textbook and have a clean copy of the essay to read.

Task 2. Segment Text. Divide the essay into segments and bracket them. Keep the number of segments between 10 and 15.

Task 3. Number Segments. Number each segment and write those numbers on a separate sheet of paper. Remember to allow plenty of space to write about each segment; if possible, have no more than two segments per page. You will use this numbered paper to document observations and information about the corresponding segments.

STRATEGY 2. BRAINSTORM ABOUT TITLE

Task 1. Review. Quickly review what you know about Rosario Castellanos as a person and as a writer. Also review what you have learned about the purpose and format of the essay as a literary form.

Task 2. Brainstorm. Keeping in mind the information from Task 1, brainstorm about the title of the essay. What might it be about? Will it be satirical or realistic? What kind of essay might it be, and what purpose might it have? Document your observations on a word wheel.

 Share your speculations with your study group.

STRATEGY 3. SKIM TEXT FOR MAIN IDEA

Task 1. Skim Each Segment. Working through one segment at a time, skim for the main idea. Make notes on the numbered paper you created to correspond with each segment. Document the people mentioned and the ideas presented. Write one or two sentences for each segment. Be sure to make note of the relevant lines in the text so that you can substantiate your observations.

STRATEGY 4. BRAINSTORM AND SPECULATE

Task 1. Compare. With your study group, compare your notes and observations from Strategy 3. Make sure everyone provides textual support to substantiate the observations.

Task 2. Elaborate. Elaborate on your own observations with the information provided by your study group.

Task 3. Brainstorm and Speculate. As a group, brainstorm about the main idea of the essay. Then look at the results from Strategy 2, Task 2, in which you brainstormed about the title. Speculate on what the essayist is striving to say to whom. Who is the target audience?

Stage III. First Reading

Objective:

- To scan for specific grammatical and textual elements that provide basic information about the essay

This stage relies on recognition of linguistic elements to foster the first level of comprehension of the text. This is the fact-finding stage. It is important to keep your information well organized.

STRATEGY 1. ANALYZE FIRST AND FINAL SEGMENTS

Task 1. Analyze First Segment. Use a fact sheet (see Appendix) to analyze the first segment of the essay. Record the verb tenses used, examples of the vocabulary, and any other information that might be important. Does the essayist pose questions or make statements? Do the adjectives create a positive or negative image?

Task 2. Analyze Final Segment. Using another fact sheet, analyze the final segment of the essay. Record the same information and ask the same questions you did in Task 1.

Task 3. Make Connections. Look back at the results of Task 1. How does the first segment relate to the title of the essay? What kind of tone does it set? What kind of information does it offer? Then do the same with the results of Task 2. Finally, compare the first segment to the final segment. How do they relate or not relate? What connections can you make between them? What kinds of closure does the final segment offer, or not offer?

———

———

———

———

Task 4. Speculate. Based on the work you have just done, what you know about the essayist, and what you know about the essay as a literary form, speculate about how the essayist will develop the issue addressed in the essay. What stance will the essayist take? To whom will the essay appeal?

———

———

———

———

STRATEGY 2. SCAN EACH SEGMENT FOR INFORMATION

Task 1. Skim. Using your segmented working copy of the essay and blank fact sheets, skim the remaining segments and add to the notes you already have. Can you expand on your observations?

Task 2. Scan for Verbs. Carefully scan each segment, making note of the most important verbs. Highlight, underline, or in some way identify those verbs.

Task 3. Scan for Pronouns. Scan each segment again, this time circling the pronouns you are able to identify. Make sure you know who is talking to whom about what.

 Task 4. Compare. With your study group, compare the results of the first three tasks and fill in any gaps that might exist.

STRATEGY 3. CREATE WORD WHEEL FOR EACH CHARACTER

Task 1. Create Word Wheel. Due to the nature and purpose of the essay, the "characters" are comprised of the author, the focus or issue, and the audience. Create a word wheel for each of these "characters" and their functions.

 Task 2. Compare. Compare your results from Task 1 with those of your study group. Can you agree on the role or function each "character" plays in the essay?

STRATEGY 4. COMPLETE STAR DIAGRAM WITH ANSWERS
TO THE "FIVE W'S"

Task 1. Scan for Information. Scan the essay and mark the words or phrases that answer the following questions.

> **Who?** The writer (**el ensayista**) and the hearer/reader (**el receptor / el lector**) of the essay
>
> **What?** The issue being addressed (**la hipótesis / las premisas**)
>
> **Where?** The historical and/or geographical context or space of the essay
>
> **When?** The chronological focus or time frame of the essay
>
> **Why?** The purpose and style of the essay (**la finalidad ensayística, la exposición, el argumento**)

Task 2. Create Star Diagram. Organize the information from Task 1 on a star diagram (see Appendix). For each "point," cite the words or phrases from the essay that substantiate your answers. Add any and all pertinent information.

STRATEGY 5. IDENTIFY INFORMATION GAPS

Task 1. Review. Review what you learned about essays in the first part of this chapter so that you know what it is you need to know in order to understand and discuss this particular literary form.

Task 2. Identify Information Gaps. Make note of the information that you did *not* uncover during Stages II and III. The information that you do not have is just as important as the information that you do. It is fine to not know something at this point, as long as you are aware of what you do know and what you still need to know.

I know: _____

_____

_____

I need to know: _____

_____

_____

Task 3. Identify Vocabulary Gaps. List any vocabulary or concept that you do not understand. It is important to begin by trying to clarify confusion on your own. Try to guess at meaning based on root words, context, and prior knowledge about story formats and similar situations. Then consult the textbook, a dictionary, and/or another classmate. Finally, ask your instructor. Write down what you learn about each vocabulary item or concept.

_____

_____

_____

_____

Stage IV. Second Reading

Objective:

- To create a thematic structure of the essay

Using the information you gathered during the pre-reading observations and the fact-finding stage, your task here is to further examine the surface structure of the text and explore the elements that make the essay an exposition or an argument.

Task 1. Ask Yourself. At this point, can you determine the format of the sample essay? Review the tasks you completed in the **Introducción al ensayo** and use them to determine your answer. Write your answer here, then come back and check it when you have finished this section.

This essay is _____ .

STRATEGY 1. REVIEW RELEVANT SYNTAX

Task 1. Decode Verbs. In previous tasks you identified the most important verbs in each segment of the essay. Decode those verbs so that you know who does what to whom, and record the information on a Verbal Elements chart (see Appendix).

Share your work with your study group. You all should have the same information about the verbs. Discuss and remedy any discrepancies.

Task 2. Transfer and Decode Pronouns. Transfer the pronouns you identified in the first reading. Decode them and record the information on a Pronoun Identification chart (see Appendix). Make sure that you can identify the antecedent of each pronoun.

Task 3. Compare. Share your results from Tasks 1 and 2 with your study group. Discuss the impact of the verb tenses and pronouns you identified on the overall tone of the essay.

Task 4. Decode Sentences. Use a Parts of Speech chart (see Appendix) to decode the sentences that contain the verbs and pronouns you identified in the previous tasks.

STRATEGY 2. RELATE ACTIONS TO CHARACTERS

NOTE: This strategy is applicable when the essay is **un ensayo poético, un ensayo dramático,** or **un ensayo narrativo.** If that is the case, complete the following tasks.

Task 1. Create Word Wheel. Create a word wheel for each "character" in the essay and record the information related to that character. Focus on the character's function in the essay. What does the character do to deliver the essayist's message? What perspective does the character provide? Support the entries on your word wheels with specific textual references.

Task 2. Compare and Contrast. If applicable, document the relationship between the characters using a venn diagram (see Appendix) to indicate the similarities and differences both in who they are and what they do.

 Compare your findings with your study group.

Study Hint: Recognizing Essays

In order to understand the essay as a literary form, it is important to be able to recognize one when you see or hear it, and to be able to identify the literary devices that the essayist used to accomplish his/her goal. Designate a block of time during which you will analyze everything verbal and written you encounter for its expository or argumentative devices. Drawing on what you have learned so far, determine what you will attend to before you begin your analysis, including the rhetorical clues you will look for. Report your most interesting findings to your study group and/or the rest of your class. You might be surprised at how often in our daily lives we are, knowingly and unknowingly, verbally or nonverbally, brought into the essayist's "dialogue" about issues of the world around us.

STRATEGY 3. SUMMARIZE EACH SEGMENT

Task 1. Identify Topic Sentence. Using your working copy of the essay, bracket or underline the topic sentence(s) of each segment. If there is no clear topic sentence, invent one and write it in the margin next to the segment.

Task 2. Delete Information. Skim your working copy, segment by segment, and draw a line through redundant information or information that is not relevant to the focus and purpose of the essay.

Task 3. Generalize. Look at the information left in the segment. Can it be generalized?

Task 4. Summarize. Based on the results of Tasks 1, 2, and 3, summarize the segments and determine the format and function of the essay. Is it expository or argumentative?

Task 5. Check Yourself. Go back to the beginning of this stage. What essay format did you guess? Were you right?

STRATEGY 4. CREATE THEMATIC STRUCTURE

Task 1. Identify Thematic Elements. Review Tasks 1–9 on pages 98–100, where you explored the elements that an essayist can use to develop **la exposición** or **el argumento.** Identify in the essay the elements that the essayist uses to develop his or her perspective (**los silogismos, los teoremas, los axiomas**). Extract the statements in the essay that represent those elements.

Task 2. Complete Thematic Structure. Enter the information from Task 1 into a sequence chain (see Appendix). Each link in the sequence chain should reflect the logical train of thought the essayist employs in order to develop the focus of the essay from the beginning to the end.

 Task 3. Compare. Compare your results from Task 2 with your study group. Everyone should have ended up with a similar sequence chain, although some may differ slightly because of personal perspectives or interpretations. Whatever you write down, be ready to substantiate and

support your point of view. If there are major differences, trace your answers back to their textual sources, discuss them with your study group, and determine the more appropriate answer.

NOTE: Upon completing these four stages, you have fulfilled your responsibility as the reader of the essay. The information you have extracted from the essay has prepared you to contribute intelligently to any discussion. If you really have absorbed the elements of the essay, you will be able to employ them in your own contributions to the discussions about the essay. How might you persuade your classmates or your instructor to accept your point of view?

D. WRITING AND OTHER DIVERSIONS

This section offers a variety of tasks and activities that your instructor can assign, you can do on your own, or you can do with your study group. The more you apply and use your new knowledge, the better you will store it for later retrieval. It is also important to find ways in which you can have fun with your new skills and knowledge.

- Create a visual representation of the different types of essay formats. Brainstorm examples of each type.

  - Group-write an essay with your study group. One person writes down a hypothesis and passes the paper to the next person, who adds to the first person's contribution, then passes the paper on. This continues until someone provides the conclusion. Evaluate your essay as a group and revise, elaborate, and edit where necessary.
- Working individually, develop one product of your group-write into a polished essay.
- An effective persuasive speech begins with a "hook," that is, a creative statement that catches the attention of the audience. The "hook" can be a story, a quote, a statement, a question, a list of words, an image, a visualization, a play on words, or some type of nonverbal communication. Select three topics in which you have a great interest and create a different "hook" for each of them.

  - With your study group, select several topics and create "hooks" for each of them, experimenting with the different types of "hooks" mentioned.

- Expand a "hook" from the previous activity into an essay and present it to the class.
- Read an essay out loud, as if you were the essayist speaking to an audience. Remember that your voice is your most powerful tool.
- "Interview" an essayist for a talk show or magazine. What would you ask and what would he or she answer?
- For several days, try to find examples of as many types of essays as you can in your daily life. Keep track of when and where you see them, as well as the type of essay you see. Present your favorite(s) to the class.
- Pick a topic that is important to you and write an essay about it. If you did the first activity in this section you can use your visual representations to guide you.
- Pick an issue that does *not* interest you or with which you disagree, and write a persuasive essay in support of it. (**Variation:** Write two essays, one in support of the issue and one against.)
- Pick a famous person and write an essay on a topic relevant to that person as if you were that person.

Read your essay out loud to your study group and see if they can guess who you are.

Appendix

VENN DIAGRAM

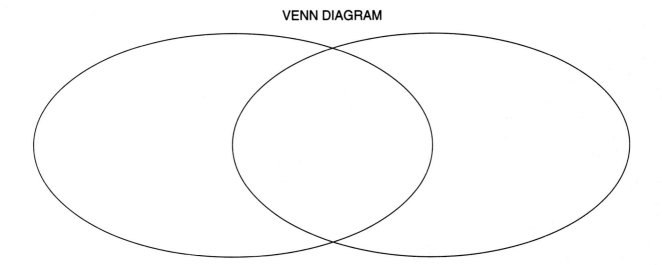

EVENTOS	NARRATIVA	POESÍA		DRAMA	ENSAYO
		SIGLO			

WORD WHEEL

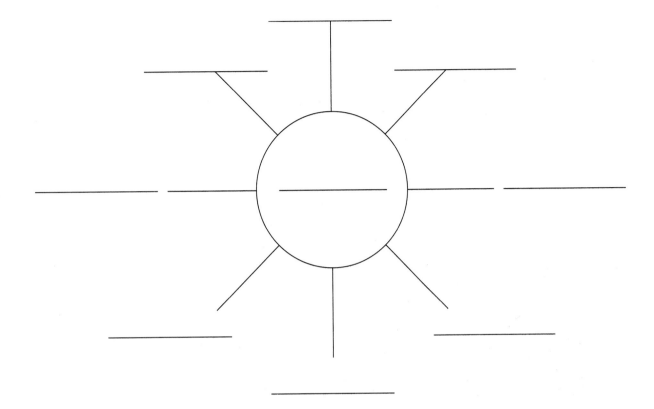

FACT SHEET

Title: _____

Segment # _____

Verb Tenses	Vocabulary	General Information

_____

_____

_____

_____

_____

_____

_____

_____

_____

_____

_____

_____

_____

_____

Additional information or observations: _____

_____

_____

_____

_____

_____

_____

STAR DIAGRAM

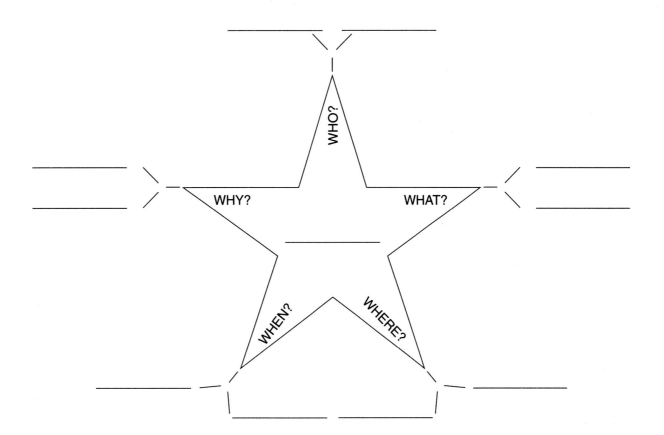

VERBAL ELEMENTS

Text: _____

VERB	Infinitive	Root	Person	Number	Mood	Tense	English Equivalent
1.							
2.							
3.							
4.							
5.							
6.							
7.							
8.							
9.							
10.							

PARTS OF SPEECH

Text: _____

Subject	Verb	D.O.	I.O.	Other
1.				
2.				
3.				
4.				
5.				
6.				
7.				
8.				
9.				
10.				

PRONOUN IDENTIFICATION

Text: _____

Line No.	Pronoun	Antecedent	Function
_____	_____	_____	_____
_____	_____	_____	_____
_____	_____	_____	_____
_____	_____	_____	_____
_____	_____	_____	_____
_____	_____	_____	_____
_____	_____	_____	_____
_____	_____	_____	_____
_____	_____	_____	_____
_____	_____	_____	_____
_____	_____	_____	_____
_____	_____	_____	_____
_____	_____	_____	_____

CHARACTER/EVENT/TRAIT DIAGRAM

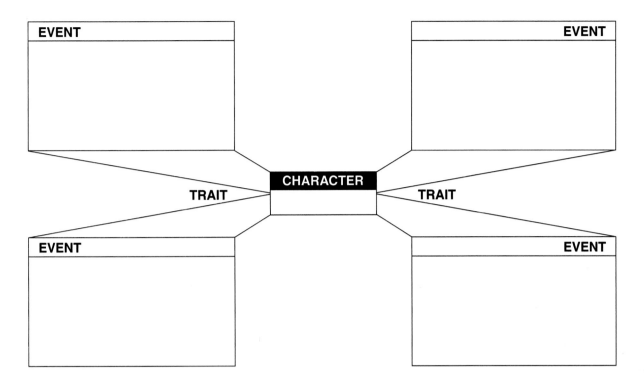

Sequence Chain for

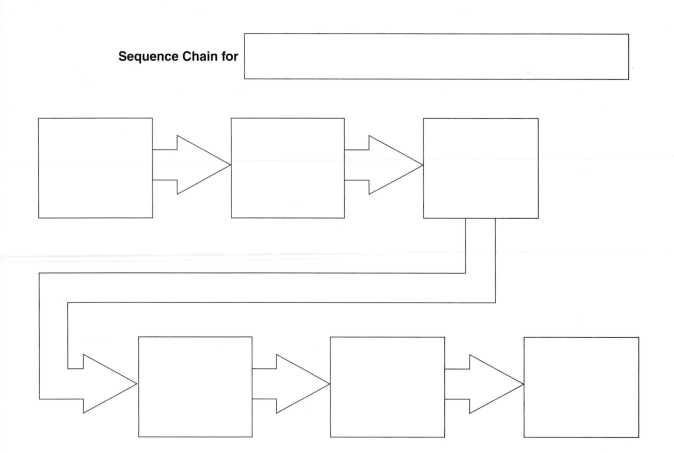

STORY MAP

Title: _____

Setting:

Characters: _____   _____

_____   _____

_____   _____

Problem:

Event 1 _____

Event 2 _____

Event 3 _____

Event 4 _____

Event 5 _____

Solution:

THEMATIC STRUCTURE

Title of poem: —————————————————————————

Name of poet: —————————————————————————

Thematic thread	Literary language

Beginning verses ————————————————————————

Middle verses ————————————————————————

End verses ————————————————————————